# WHAT IS MAN?

## Herb Hodges

# WHAT IS MAN?

### Herb Hodges – author

Copyright @ 2010 by Spiritual Life Ministries. All rights reserved. No part of this book may be reproduced or transmitted in any form or by any means without prior written permission from Spiritual Life Ministries, except for brief passages quoted in articles or reviews.

All Scripture quotations, unless otherwise indicated are taken from the King James Version.

**Spiritual Life Ministries**
**2916 Old Elm Lane**
**Germantown, TN 38138**
*E-mail: herbslm@mindspring.com*

ISBN: 978-0-9829957-0-9

Printed in the United States of America

Other titles written by Herb Hodges and available through Spiritual Life Ministries:

*Tally Ho the Fox – The Foundation for Building World-Visionary, World-Impacting, Reproducing Disciples*

*Fox Fever—Exploring both the Will and the Skill to obey Christ's Great Commission to "turn people into disciples"*

*The Outrageous Love of God – A series of Studies on the Pearl of Parables in Luke 15*

# AUTHOR'S PREFACE

Two completely diverse worldviews have locked horns in furious battle in the philosophical world, and each of them is firm in its stance about man. The tug-of-war over man is a major battle, and much is at stake. The side which each person chooses will determine the quality of His present life and contribution as well as the destiny that is consequent to his choice. To paraphrase Jesus, "One man's story is indelibly written on the rock, while the other is written in sand." That which bears the stamp of God is eternal, but that which is merely man's product will quickly dissipate on the near shore of eternity. The immediate choices that reflect the two views are crucial and the eternal destinies fashioned by them are final and forever. One is the Christian view of man and things, the other is the humanist or naturalist (atheistic) view of man and things. The Christian view will finally emerge as victor because God is its Source and Sponsor. We tend to think of the other side merely as a secular, humanist view, but this is far too simplistic to a Christian. The "other side" is determined by the natural minds of multitudes of men and the nefarious minds of Satan and his forces. These two categorical minds often act in close conjunction with each other, though no secularist would admit a supernatural source as the initiator of his views. "The god of this world has blinded the minds of those who believe not, lest the light of the glorious Gospel of Christ, who is the image of God, should shine unto them" (II Corinthians 4:4). This determines the secular, humanist, atheistic mind, which is, believe it or not, more a moral and spiritual response than it is an academic determination. "God, who commanded the light to shine out of darkness, hath shined in our hearts, to give the light of the knowledge of the glory of God in the face of Jesus Christ" (II Corinthians 4:6). This determines the Christian mind.

The Christian view is that man and the universe were created by God, and that man is the image and likeness and glory of God. The humanist view is that man is the result of an accidental assembly of atoms. Man is explained either by *evolution* or by *revelation.* William Temple went the revelation route when he said, "We only know what man is when God dwells in him." Jacques Monod, humanist philosopher, cleverly pursued the other course when he wrote that man's "number came up in the Monte Carlo games", and the assumption is that man briefly plays until his "number is up." One problem with thinking of man as a mere assortment of atoms or as a thinking animal is that those who hold that view breed from their ranks increasing numbers of "leaders" who have no scruples about herding men into disposal bins and slaughtering them as cattle in a slaughterhouse. Man is *not* the master of his fate, but the one that believes that he is may assume such a superiority that he sees himself as the master of the fates of many, many others. The totalitarianism of the humanists is a logical and inexorable consequence of their humanism.

It is more than interesting to me that in our present culture, the one intolerable sin is intolerance. Every view must be tolerated today—that is, every view except the view of supernatural Christianity. The Lordship of Christ clashes sharply with the autonomy of the individual man. The one is true, the other is assumed, and never the twain shall meet. In the view of the secular humanist, Christians are guilty of the dastardly sin of believing and announcing the Biblical view of absolute truth. Backed by a mighty resurrection from the dead, Jesus Christ said, "You shall know the truth, and the truth shall set you free." The most gratifying life I can imagine is the life I have found as a dependent man exercising personal and relational faith in Jesus Christ as the Lord of my life. That surrender certainly has not made me less of a man, or a slave, but as I honor Him as Lord and enjoy relationship with Him, He has given me the only real freedom I have ever known. I know many, many, many such Christians, and I have never heard a single expression of regret or disappointment from any of them regarding personal relationship with Christ. Indeed, they are eager to lovingly share their testimonies with those who do not have such a relationship and seek to bring them into "the relational knowledge of Him." G. K. Chesterton, the brilliant British Christian philosopher and writer, once said, "If man never suspects what a noble creature he was meant to be, he will never see what a deprived and depraved creature he is." If man ever sees the glorious potential in himself, and realizes who installed it there and who alone can really develop it and deploy it in a maximum way within and through the man, he will be far more eager to seriously consider the claims of Christ and give Him His proper place in his life. It is my hope that this little volume of assorted truths about man will aid in that consideration. Some of the ideas in the book are debatable and questionable, which is the case with most any book. I do not hold my ideas as a necessarily final dogma, because I am subject to correction by more light and better understanding of The Truth—but I do want to be always moving toward the light. "Further up and further in," as C. S. Lewis said. As I continue the ascent, I pray that you will join me and we will be mutually gratified by His wonderful grace. May you be blessed and encouraged as you read.

- Herb Hodges –

# Table of Contents

Author's Preface . . . . . . . . . . . . . . . . . . .. . . . . . . . 3

1. The Meaning of Man . . . . . . . . . . . . . . . . .. . . . . . . 8
   *Psalms 8:3-9, Hebrews 2:5-9*

2. The Making of Man .. . . . . . . . . .. . . . . . .. . . . . 28
   *Genesis 1:26-27*

3. The Marriage and Mating of Man . . . . . . . . . . . . 46
   *Genesis 2:18-24*

4. The Makeup of Man . . . . . . . . . . . . . . . . . . . . . . . . . 66
   *I Thessalonians 5:23*

5. The Misery of Man . . . . . . . . . . . . . . . . . . . ….. . . . . . 88
   *Genesis 3:1-24*

6. The Measure of Man . . . . . . . . .. . . . . . . . . . ….. . . . . 118
   *II Corinthians 10:12, 17-18*

7. The Mercy for Man . . . . . . . . . . . . . . . . .. . . . . 138
   *Jeremiah 17:9, Colossians 2:13-15; II Cors. 3:1-3*

8. The Master for Man . . . . . . . . . . . . . . . . . . . . . . . . 168
   *John 13:13*

9. The Magnitude of Man .. . . … . . . . . . . . . . …. . . . . 184
   *Jeremiah 18:1-6*

10. *The Motto for Man* .. . . . . . . . . . . . . . . . . . . …... . . . . 202
    *Philippians 1:21*

11. SO, WHAT IS MAN? . . . . . . . . . . . . . . . . . . . . . . . . 222

Appendix – Chapter Outlines . . . . . . . . . . . . . . . . .. 236

*Chapter 1*

# THE MEANING OF MAN

*"When I consider thy heavens, the work of thy fingers, the moon and the stars, which thou hast ordained; What is man, that thou art mindful of him? And the son of man, that thou visitest him? For thou hast made him a little lower than the angels, and hast crowned him with glory and honor. Thou madest him to have dominion over the works of thy hands; thou hast put all things under his feet: All sheep and oxen, yea, and the beasts of the field; The fowl of the air, and the fish of the sea, and whatsoever passeth through the paths of the seas. O LORD our Lord, how excellent is thy name in all the earth! (Psalm 8:3-9)*

*"Unto the angels hath he not put in subjection the world to come, whereof we speak. But one in a certain place testified, saying, What is man, that thou art mindful of him? Or the son of man, that thou visitest him? Thou madest him a little lower than the angels; thou crownedst him with glory and honor, and didst set him over*

*the works of thy hands: Thou hast put all things in subjection under his feet. For in that he put all in subjection under him, he left nothing that is not put under him. But now we see not yet all things put under him. But we see Jesus, who was made a little lower than the angels for the suffering of death, crowned with glory and honor; that he by the grace of God should taste death for every man."* (Hebrews 2:5-9)

Two birds sat on the ground and watched as a young frog hopped over to a nearby tree and proceeded to slowly, agonizingly climb the tree. When the frog finally reached a high limb of the tree, it crawled tediously out on the limb, stood up, spread its short front legs, and dived out into the air, desperately flailing the air with its legs—only to "splat" on the ground beneath. After it had gotten its breath again and recovered itself from the fall as much as it could, it slowly began to repeat the process— with the same result. After this happened several more times, one of the birds leaned over to the other and said firmly, "I don't care *what* you say; I'm going to *tell* him that he's *adopted!*" An awareness of *self-identity, capability* and *limitations* is all-important!

Alexander Pope once said, "The proper study of mankind is man." However, if a man only studies himself, he may be an intelligent anthropologist, but at the same time totally ignorant of the greatest subject of all, Who is God and what is man's relationship with Him? Indeed, his study of anthropology may only cement him in his self-centeredness, fostering the view that "man is the measure of all things." What a shock awaits the human being whose perspective ends within himself and whose view of humankind is one of isolation, independence—and ignorance of ultimate truth!

A brilliant college professor was being ferried across the Mississippi River on a fairly small boat. The professor, conscious of his own superiority over his fellow travelers on the boat, said to the oarsman, "Sir, do you know anything about *history*?" "Not much," the simple man replied. "Then, probably *one-fourth of your life is gone*," the proud professor said. After a moment, the professor added this question: "Do you know anything about *the sciences*?" "Nope," was the reply. "Then *half of your life is probably gone.*" After a moment, the professor asked again, "Do you know anything about *mathematics?*" The poor man quietly replied, "No, sir, I don't." "Then *three-fourths* of your life is gone!" said the teacher. At that moment, the boat struck a snag in the river and was overturned in the swift current. As the passengers surfaced, the boatman shouted to the professor, "Sir, can you swim?" "No!" gasped the struggling professor. "Then, sir, I think *your whole life may be gone!*" The moral of the story? You can major on a lot of things which *you* think are important, but they are not ultimately important at all. The one thing that counts is your relationship with God. And please understand that I am talking about a *real, viable, vital, living, determinative relationship with God*—not just something that religious people tend to believe. A man may be intellectually brilliant in any other field, but if sterile of relationship with God, the day will come when he realizes that *his whole life is gone.*

Let me begin this examination of man with a few basic foundational Biblical truths about man. (1) Man is a *creature of God*. (2) As created, man is *complex* in nature. (3) Man, already complex by creation, has been further *complicated* by sin and corruption, and thus may be puzzling in character, concept and conduct. (4) Man is *convertible*, or *changeable*. This last truth makes very significant the description of Christian salvation in

Hebrews 2:3 as "so great salvation," because this salvation (truly experienced) has always miraculously and massively changed its recipients. Man really is convertible; I am walking evidence of the power and joy of that statement, power and joy which are found only in receiving, trusting, knowing, walking with, and serving, Jesus Christ.

The study of man is called "anthropology," which is a testimony in itself. The word is a derivative from the Greek word for man, which is *"anthropos."* This is a compound word, meaning, "the upstanding one," or the "upward looking one." So let me suggest that we keep an eye out for *ourselves* in this study, all the while focusing on *the One who is above us*. Also, let us remember the words of a wise Christian: "God and man have business with each other, and neither of them is satisfied until they are both about that business."

## I. Understand His Person

First, if we are to understand man, we must understand his *person*. That is, we must understand the nature and structure of his being.

From a Biblical perspective, man is a tripartite being. He is a "trinity," somewhat like God is. He is made of three significant "parts." In what may be the first letter chronologically of all of Paul's New Testament letters, he wrote near the end of the letter these words, "And the very God of peace sanctify you wholly; and I pray God your whole spirit and soul and body be preserved blameless unto the coming of our Lord Jesus Christ." Then, because he realized how idealistic and perhaps unrealistic this might sound to his readers, he added, "Faithful is He who called you, who also will do it" (I Thessalonians 5:23-24).

Note the three "parts" of man suggested in this verse, and note the order in which they are presented. The three parts of man are his *pneuma*, or spirit, his *psuche*, or soul, and his *soma*, or body. People who are more students of *anthropology* than students of *theology* will likely have their own view of the nature and structure of man—and some of the reduced views lead to tragic consequences for both the proponent and his students. But if his light leaves him with one of these limited views, he has difficulty agreeing with the One whose light takes him all the way to the end of the journey. Personally, I am perfectly satisfied that the Biblical view of man answers to all situations and covers all the necessities of his relationship with God *and everything else.*

The first mentioned part of man is his *pneuma*, or "spirit." His spirit is the God-created "compartment" within man which is his organ of relationship with God. Man receives Eternal Life, God's own Life in his inner character, the moment the Holy Spirit of God re-inhabits the human spirit of man, which was earlier vacated when Adam sinned. The moment of that sin, the human spirit, the compartment God had inhabited within Adam since his creation, was suddenly emptied of its Divine Occupant. At this moment, the living God moved out of the human spirit—and it became a Death Chamber within the man. This is what the Bible means when it says that human beings without Christ are *"dead in trespasses and sins" (Ephesians 2:1).* Now, it must be remembered that there is never such a thing as *total death* taught in the Bible. When a person's *body* dies, the person himself moves elsewhere, *but he continues to exist.* When a sinner is "dead in trespasses and sins," his body and soul may be alive and (apparently) well, but his spirit, the organ of relationship with God, is *dead.* Let me repeat: his spirit is *stone dead toward God*, though he may be reasonably healthy in his body and reasonably "happy" in his soul. Note that the spirit of man is mentioned first because it is by far the most important part of the individual. The eternal destiny of both his soul and body will be totally determined by the spiritual condition of his spirit. If he becomes alive to God through a new birth, the "being born again" that Jesus and other New Testament writers mentioned, then his soul and his (new, resurrection, glorified) body will go with his live spirit to Heaven. But if his spirit is "dead" toward God, that is, if no vital relationship exists between the person and God, then his body and soul will go with his dead spirit to Hell. This is serious business, indeed!

According to the Bible, there are four kinds of people on planet earth at any time. These four people are mentioned in I Corinthians 2:14-3:3. Let me briefly mention and describe them.

The first man (I Corinthians 2:14) is called "the natural man" (literally, the *psuchikos* man). The Greek word, *psuchikos*, is derived from the word, *psuche*, the word for "soul." The word *psuchikos* is a Greek adjective which means, *"adapted to soul."* So *"the natural man"* is a man who is adapted to his soul *because his spirit is dead and thus his only inner resource for living is his soul.* This man just "does what comes *naturally"* (he lives *soulishly),* because he has *no supernatural life*, no relationship with God. Because his spirit is dead, he cannot live "spiritually" in a Biblical way. This is the lost man who is devoid of God and His Life and will spend eternity getting what he wanted, independence of God. The first man mentioned is the **non-Christian** man.

The second man mentioned (I Corinthians 2:15) is called "he that is spiritual." Here, the Greek word is *pneumatikos*, which is a Greek adjective meaning, *"adapted to the spirit."* Please note carefully the real and radical difference between this man and the "natural" man. This man has been "born of the Spirit," "born again," "born from above" in a real, revolutionary, relational birth in which the Holy Spirit has literally re-entered his previously dead spirit and quickened it with the very Life of God. In that moment, the person received Eternal Life, that very quality of Life which God lives. At the moment of the person's new birth, his body and soul may not be greatly changed, but a revolutionary divine change has occurred in his spirit. Not only has this man been born of the Spirit in his own human spirit, but his entire life has taken on a new priority and a new vocation, to "grow in the Spirit" and become like Christ. These must not be taken merely as visionary and unrealistic ideals, but as realities which will occur in his lifetime as he cooperates with the indwelling Holy Spirit. The second man mentioned is the **normal Christian** man.

The third man mentioned (I Corinthians 3:1) is called "carnal." The word used here is *sarkinos*. Note that the "natural" man is *psuchikos*, the man "adapted to his soul" because his spirit is dead and his only inner resource is his soul. Note that the "spiritual" man is *pneumatikos*, the man "adapted to his spirit," because his spirit is alive and is dominant over his soul in his experience and lifestyle. Thus, his human spirit, indwelt by the Holy Spirit, controls both his soul and his body, and he is called "spiritual." The "carnal" man, however, is controlled by his *sarx*, or his *"flesh,"* which is the combination of his body and soul acting independently of the Holy Spirit. The "flesh" is everything a human being receives by his *first* birth, in which his spirit is dead. Also, note that the word in this case is *not* *"sarkikos,"* but a very close similarity, *"sarkinos."* The difference in spelling is hardly noticeable, a "k" in the first and an "n" in the second, but the meaning is substantially different between the two words. The word "sarkinos" describes a new-born Christian, a spiritual baby which has just been born, and thus is still more baby than mature believer. Like any baby believer, though this person is saved, he lives a "baby" Christian life with a baby's self-curl, self-centeredness, and self-seeking. It is reasonable that he should do so, because he *is a baby in Christ* (see I Corinthians 3:1c). So the third person mentioned is the **new-born Christian.**

The fourth man mentioned (I Corinthians 3:3) is also called "carnal," but this is a slightly different word. Whereas one "carnal" person (carnal # 1) is called *sarkinos*, "fleshly," because he is born as a self-centered baby, though actually and truly born, the other "carnal" person (carnal # 2) is called *sarkikos*, also "fleshly" but with a different time-frame, because he *has remained a baby a long time after his birth.* So one "carnal" person could be called *good* carnal, and the other (one we are most familiar with because of our teaching) could be called *bad* carnal. What is the difference between the two? Simply this: the first one is a baby and *can't* be anything else—because he has just been born! This baby is a wonderful thing! But the second one is still a baby years after being born, and he *won't* be anything else. One (*sarkinos*) is a *wonderful spiritual baby*, but the other (sarkikos) is a *willful spoiled brat*! This is the reason a Christian is commanded to "grow in grace, and in the knowledge of our Lord and Savior Jesus Christ" (II Peter 3:18). Spiritual immaturity is expected and accepted in a Christian who has just been born of the Spirit, but it is sinful in a person who has remained a baby ("protracted infancy," a sad tragedy both spiritually and physically) for years after being born again. The fourth person mentioned is the **nominal Christian** man—*God's biggest problem on earth.*

In nature, human beings are made of three parts (see I Thessalonians 5:23)—spirit, soul and body—and that Divine order reveals the order of importance of the three. The spirit, being the determinant for the others, is most important. The soul, basically a combination of mind, emotion and will, is next most important. And the body is least important of the three—though *not at all unimportant.* To show the importance of the three, if your body is right, you will be *healthy;* if your soul is right, you will be *happy;* but it is only if your spirit is right that you will be *holy.* It is God's design that you be "whole," that is, healthy, happy and holy. *"Healthy"* refers to your physical life; *"happy"* refers to your psychological (note the word *psyche,* the word for the *soul,* at the beginning of that word) life; and *"holy"* refers to your spiritual life, or the life that defines your relationship with God. *Holy* is a word that refers to your *status* with God, your *relationship* with Him, your *usefulness* to Him, and finally, your *moral character* (which will become progressively holy as you cooperate with Him). If you are only "natural" or "carnal," you cannot adequately understand man. Man can only be adequately referenced by referring to *God,* and he can only be adequately understood by a person who knows God in personal relationship with Him and cooperates with God in daily life.

Remember that man was created *complex* by nature, and he has been further *complicated* by sin and corruption. Study these things carefully, because your understanding of man and His relationship with God will be determined by them. It is important to fathom these things if we are to understand man's person.

## II. Understand His Purpose

Second, if we are to understand man, we must understand his *purpose.* Someone wisely said, "Life without purpose is merely an experiment, and without the *correct* purpose, it is misguided guesswork." Every complex product will have a "Manufacturer's Manual" with it, and the manual of operation will explain the purpose, function and operation of the product. Even so, man came attended by a Manufacturer's Manual, the Bible.

Recently I read a book by Pastor James Kennedy entitled What If the Bible Had Never Been Written? I read very little that was new to me but it was a glorious reaffirmation of something that was instantaneously, deeply, richly implanted in me at the moment of my salvation (58 years ago now!), that the Bible is the very Word of God, and that it contains the meaning, purpose, regulations, and sustenance for my existence as a Christian. My Bible has become the most valuable tangible possession which I own. In fact, a poor lost sinner could *never (never)* know the riches and resources that I find every single day of my life in my Bible. It is an actual treasure trove of wealth to a Spirit-walking Christian. Furthermore, though I have read it many times, each reading opens new "vaults" of riches to me. You see, when the "living Word of God" (John 1:1, 14), Jesus Christ, comes into a human being, He brings His own taste for the *written Word of God* with Him. So I have Christ in me, operating with His own taste for the written Word of God, so I eat the Word, governed by *His taste for it.* Job 23:12 says, "I have treasured the words of His mouth more than my necessary food"; *I understand and agree with that testimony!* Jeremiah 15:16 says, "Thy words were found, and I did eat them; and thy word was unto me the joy and rejoicing of my heart: for I am called by thy name, O LORD God of hosts." As the old mountaineer said, "Them's my sentiments, 'zactly!" A Spirit-walking Christian "has meat to eat that they (the world) know nothing about," but the Christian knows that he is made healthy by that "meat" while the rest of the world spiritually starves to death!

This Manufacturer's Manual, the Bible, tells man what his purpose is. The purpose of anything is that overwhelming, most important reason for which it exists. The purpose of a thing cannot be discovered by asking another thing. Only the Manufacturer (!) knows why He (!) created the product the way He did. Whether you know it or not, my friend, God is your Manufacturer, and He gave you life and endowed you with personality with a Manufacturer's Design in mind—and He simply cannot disregard the travesty if you willfully ignore His Design in favor of your own guesses. You may be sure of this: the "machine" will never run satisfactorily if you ignore the plan of the Maker! This leaves you to guesswork thinking and patchwork performance, and you must remember that you are a sinner, "alienated from the life of God through the ignorance that is in you" (Ephesians 4:18). With all of your potential soulish intelligence, and even with that "intelligence" fully developed, possibly producing a very high IQ, you are still lost and dead without God—and it is very difficult for dead men to realize their own problem! If you ever come alive to God, you will realize (but only then) how dead you are/were without Him.

Nobody knows your purpose like the One who made you. You may choose to vaunt your independence and "invent" your own purpose, but just look at the present world-at-large to see the disjointedness of this.

So what is man's purpose as God has revealed it? For a suggestion of that purpose, consult the Hebrews text and context. See in Hebrews 2:7 the word "glory". The same word recurs in Hebrews 2:9 and 2:10—three times in four verses. And its use indicates the purpose of man's existence. "God crowned man with glory" (2:7); "We see Jesus ... crowned with glory" (2:9); It was God's design to finally "bring many sons unto glory" (2:10). What does this word "glory" mean? Biblically, the main use of the word "glory" is in defining something about the very nature of God. "Glory" is the character of God on display; it is the exhibit of the nature of God. The Bible says, "All have sinned, and come short of the glory (the holy character) of God" (Romans 3:23). Glory is the outshining of God's own radiance from within a container (!). For example, John 1:14, speaking of the Incarnation of Christ, says, "The Word became flesh, and dwelt among us, and we beheld His glory." The word "beheld" is the Greek word from which we get our word "theater," and it presupposes an involved examination of an object so that we become implicated in the idea and purpose of that object (like seeing a play in a theater). We get involved in the plot ourselves! *So Christians are to get involved in God's plot for revealing His own character!!!*

Hebrews 2:9 and John 1:14 reveal that the "ground zero" of God's self-revelation is in the Person of Christ, where a perfect revelation of His glory has been seen *in human flesh on earth!* Now, our purpose is to be Christ-like, the purpose for which the Manufacturer designed us (see Romans 8:29). So we too are to be display cases, or exhibit points, for His glory. *I was made to be a container, a carrier, a conveyor and communicator of the glory of God!* Do you not see, my friend, that no independent and invented purpose for man can match the Maker's Model? No self-purpose can equal the Savior's purpose. How empty such other purposes look to a Spirit-walking Christian. He sighs in pity when he sees a humanly intelligent person wasting his life on lesser purposes, and wonders what the eye-opening final judgment will look like to him after mis-spending his life seeking his selfish goals.

So human beings are made for containing Christ ("Christ in you, the guarantee of glory," Colossians 1:27), for communing with God (see Exodus 33:11 and 34:29), and for communicating His glory to others (so that they "glorify" God; see Galatians 1:24). And all of this must be done according to God's design, that is, on His terms. You see, even a Christian can make a mere generic commitment to Christ as Lord—that is, He confesses Christ as Lord with His mouth, but balks at the full demands of the Manufacturer's Manual. That Christian is, at least for the moment, "carnal," and cannot expect to know a fully gratifying and massively fruitful Christian life. "Jesus is either Lord of all (He calls all of the shots involving the devotion, dynamic, delight and distance of your commitment) or He is not Lord at all." If He is Lord of all within me, others will glorify God because of Christ-in-control-in-me, and His glory showing through me. This is the staggering and gratifying purpose for which God gave me natural life and then invaded my life in the Person of Jesus, Who is the personification of His glory.

## III. Understand His Progress

Third, if we are to understand man, we must understand his *progress.* That is, we must understand His history. If a twenty-dollar gold piece has fallen into a lake in aboriginal Australia and an Australian aborigine finds it while diving there, he would find an explanation of its history to be helpful in his attempt to understand the coin. Today, most human beings are like the lost coin in a story told by Jesus (Luke 15:8-10). It was hidden in the darkness and dirt of a dark and dirty household, and could only be found by scouring away the dirt and shining a light into the darkness. When this happens in real human experience, the "lamp" of God's Word (Psalm 119:105) and the "washing" of Christ's blood (Revelation 1:5) will allow us to examine the full history of man from God's viewpoint. Let me point out that history, step by step.

Look at the *first* man. He was *innocent* man, man as created by God (Genesis 1 and 2). Adam and Eve were created with pristine innocence and placed in a perfect environment. So man was originally *created* by God, and he was innocent. This part of man's history is suggested in Hebrews 2:6-8a.

Then, there was *fallen* man. Tragically, man became *infected* by an alien wickedness, with the infection induced by a fallen angel named Satan. Thus, man became *corrupted* by sin and guilt. This part of man's history is suggested in Hebrews 2:8b; read this sentence carefully, noting the words, "But now," and "not yet."

Third, there was *full* (and *fulfilled*) man (Man). This is the *Incarnate Man*, the God-man. This, of course, is *Christ* Himself. "God was in Christ," says II Corinthians 5:19. "It pleased the Father that in Him should all fullness dwell" (Colossians 1:19), and "in Him dwells all the fullness of the Godhead bodily" (Colossians 2:9). Jesus is the fulfillment of the Father's Original Idea for man. This is stated in Hebrews 2:9, which incidentally contains the first mention of the Name "Jesus" in the book of Hebrews.

Fourth, there is *faith-oriented* man, or the Christian. This is *indwelt* man. "Christ lives in me," Paul wrote (Galatians 2:20), and every born-again Christian echoes this testimony by his lips and his lifestyle. This is *converted* man, converted by the grace and power of God. The grace and love of God are the objective means of his conversion, and the power of God exercised in his New Birth is the subjective means of his conversion.

Finally, there is the *future* man. Then, each Christian will be the *ideal* man, the model of God's intention. This is *consummated, completed* man. Theology calls him "the glorified man," or man with a resurrected, glorified body and reflecting Christ's glory each moment of eternity. This is suggested in Hebrews 2:10, which speaks of "many sons of God brought to glory."

This then is the history of man—the *first* man, then *fallen*, then ideally *fulfilled* in the Person of Christ, then the *faith-oriented*, born-again, saved man, and finally, the *future* glorified man. Each of these steps in man's history must be understood if we are to answer the question, "What is man?"

## IV. Understand His Potential

Finally, if we are to understand man, we must understand his *potential.* It is my firm conviction that one of the greatest sins a human being can commit is the sin of unfulfilled potential. Furthermore, this sin is common and flagrant among Christians, and it is a sin which surely deeply grieves the Holy Spirit. When the profile of the Christian life revealed in the New Testament is placed before me, and I see the disparity, the discrepancy, the difference, the *contrast* between what it says and what I am, what I think, what I say and do, I realize that I have left a vast stockpile of potential latent within me, yet undeveloped and unexploited.

Long ago, I heard this statement about Christian commitment: "One who does condemns all of those who don't." I heard this statement in the context of the Biblical story of Enoch (Genesis 5:21-24), the man whose entire biography was recorded in four words, "Enoch walked with God." The speaker applied his adage to Enoch in these words, "When Enoch walked with God, he both reflected the Divine ideal for every man, and revealed the possibility for every man to *walk with God. And sadly, he* exposed the perversion of every person who does not walk with God. Since Enoch walked with God, he condemns all of those who don't walk with God."

All of the offers, all of the opportunities, all of the claims, all of the commands of the Gospel which God extends to man are offers and opportunities to develop man's latent potential. When God speaks, the door of possibility springs open. When God communicates an assignment, He also offers an endowment to complete it. His communication of an assignment is always attended by a matching communication of ability. The responsibility is always accompanied by the resources to complete it—if we whole-heartedly, and wholly, obey. When I practically pursue God's guidance, I personally partake of His providence. Where He practically reigns, He powerfully sustains.

Let me state a practical test which I/you can apply personally. Have I deliberately determined to understand the full nature and responsibility of being a Christian? Am I daily searching the Scriptures to be sure I am fully understanding what is expected of me as a Christian? Are there dimensions of the Biblical revelation that I have ignored—either deliberately or indifferently? Since the Bible is such a replete Book, am I being fair to the full dimensions and demands of it? Practically, am I showing evidence of a present-tense salvation in my life today—that is, are there evidences that Jesus is "saving me" today in an ongoing way? Is real sanctification—the continuing development of a holy life—occurring in me daily? Is Christian service, the "work of ministering" (Ephesians 4:12) to which God has called *each Christian*, visible on a daily basis in my life?

You see, many of us are carrying vast undeveloped potential toward our graves. I wonder how God will measure the return on that investment He made in us.

Let me conclude by mentioning two areas of potential which characterize every human being. I am deeply persuaded that God fully expects a massive return from each of us because of the vast potential He has placed in us in these areas.

The first is the area of *Divine indwelling—the fullness of God's Presence.* Originally, God made man to be a container, a carrier, a conveyor, of His Person, of His Presence. God made a "compartment" deep within Adam and Eve that was intended to be His place of occupancy. As mentioned earlier in this study, this is called the "spirit" of man. God's Holy Spirit dwelt in this human spirit of man from the moment of Adam's creation, and God's intent was to display Himself through the human being. This meant that the Holy Spirit could control the soul and the body of Adam from His place of occupancy in Adam's human spirit, and thus God could release His very Life into Adam's surroundings. So any observer could see both man and God by looking at Adam. What a testimonial to God's purpose and power, that he could make such a creature and then use him to display His glory!

Though man has been corrupted by sin since the Fall of Adam, God's Original Purpose has not been altered. It is still His design to occupy each man, own each man, and operate each man to give him Abundant Life and the opportunity to make Him and that Life known to every intelligent being in His universe. But the Bible clearly teaches that, since the Fall of man, only the redeemed and restored person (the Christian) can realize this ideal—and even then, it will be realized only as we understand that ideal and cooperate with Him in reaching toward it. In fact, the potential will only partially be realized in any man.

For a Christian, this ideal is powerfully expressed in a great passage in Ephesians 3:14-19, which says (Amplified Bible), "For this reason (seeing the greatness of this plan), I bow my knees before the Father of our Lord Jesus Christ, For Whom every family in heaven and on earth is named (that Father from whom all fatherhood takes its title and derives its name). May He grant you out of the rich treasure of His glory to be strengthened and reinforced with mighty power in the inner man by the Holy Spirit (Himself indwelling your innermost being and personality). May Christ through your faith (actually) dwell (settle down, abide, make His permanent home) in your hearts! May you be rooted deep in love and founded securely on love, That you may have the power and be strong to apprehend and grasp with all saints (God's devoted people), what is the breadth and length and height and depth (of that love); (that you may really come) to know (practically, through experience for yourselves) the love of Christ, which far surpasses mere knowledge, that you may be filled (through all your being) unto all the fullness of God (may have the richest measure of the divine Presence, and become a body wholly filled and flooded with God Himself)!"

Read the preceding paragraph several times, and realize that this is one area of the staggering potential of every Christian—to be filled and controlled by all the fullness of God. Admit that this is a real possibility for you, and open the doors of faith in your inner spirit so that God can absolutely fill and flood you with His Presence.

The other area I would mention which exposes man's potential is this: *the fulfillment of God's highest purpose.* I can fulfill the very purpose for which God created man—practicing full devotion, engaging fully in "the work of ministering," exploiting His resources to fulfill my responsibility, and going the full distance (yes, geographically—to "the uttermost part of the earth) by implementing His strategy.

So I -- puny, pusillanimous, pygmy me, can be "filled with all the fullness of the Presence of God," and can fulfill in a massive and productive way the very Purpose for which He created me and saved me.

If I am to understand man, if I am to answer the question, "What is man?" I must understand man's person, understand his purpose, understand His progressive history, and understand his potential. Lord, teach me who/what I am, teach me the purpose of my existence from Your standpoint, and teach me my vast potential, which, when fulfilled, will bring great glory to You and great good to multitudes.

If I am reaching a non-Christian person by these words, let me have a few last seconds with him (you). Dear friend, Jesus Christ loves you with an unmerited, unlimited love, and He wants you in His Family of faith. You may enter that Family today by these simple procedures:

Confess your sins and your need directly to Him, admitting that you have sinned against Him (Psalm 51:4). Up to this point, you have not been a mere neutral human being, but a sinner whose sins place you into warfare with Him.

Remember that He loves you, not because you are so loveable, but because He is love and cannot violate His own nature.

Remember, too, that He died for you as if you were the only sinner who ever lived. If you had been the only human being, and lost in sin, He would have died the same qualitative death for you that He died for all.

Recognize that the Bible says that He died and rose again from the dead, sealing His victory over sin, and death, and Hell, and that if you will trust Him, the Risen and Living Christ, to save you, He will literally enter your life, instantly forgive all of your sins, and give you the gift of Eternal Life—His own Life. The next breath you breathe, the next thought you have, the next step you take, will be the beginning of a New Life in Him. You may take it from me, a wonderfully "satisfied customer," that Jesus will be the best Friend you have ever known. ***Trust Him today!***

*Chapter 2*

# THE MAKING OF MAN

*"And God said, Let us make man in our image, after our likeness: and let them have dominion over the fish of the sea, and over the fowl of the air, and over the cattle, and over all the earth, and over every creeping thing that creepeth upon the earth. So God created man in his own image, in the image of God created He him; male and female created He them." "And the LORD God formed man of the dust of the ground, and breathed into his nostrils the breath of life; and man became a living soul." (Genesis 1:26-27; 2:7)*

Two scientists were discussing the dimensions and dynamics of man's being. One said, "Astronomically speaking, man is the essence of insignificance." The other retorted, "Perhaps so, but astronomically speaking, *man is the astronomer.*" Without a Biblical frame, the picture we hold of man is pitiful, indeed. Without a Biblical anthropology (doctrine of man), our faith about man is almost forced to be *unbelief.* Without a relationship with God, man is very likely to look and act like a devil. So we turn again to the Bible to understand man.

The one event that upstages everything else in the first chapter of Genesis is the creation of man. Genesis one is a chapter of "firsts", but the most important one is the creation of the first man.

Job made his own creation a matter of testimony about God. "The Spirit of God has made me, and the breath of the Almighty has given me life" (Job 33:4). David spoke generically when he said, "Know ye that the Lord He is God; it is He who has made us, and not we ourselves" (Psalm 100:3). Referring to mankind, Proverbs 22:2 says, "The Lord is the maker of them all." In I Corinthians 11:7, the theologian/Apostle Paul wrote, "Man is the image and glory of God."

In one of the greatest and most timely sermons ever preached, a sermon entitled "The Weight of Glory," C.S. Lewis said, "It is a serious thing to live in a society of possible gods and goddesses, to remember that the dullest and most uninteresting person you talk to may one day be a creature which, if you saw it now, you would be strongly tempted to worship, or else a horror and corruption such as you now meet, if at all, only in a nightmare. All day long we are, in some degree, helping each other to one or other of these destinations. Even our merriment must be of a kind which exists between people who have, from the beginning, taken each other seriously. Next to the things of the Holy Gospel, your neighbor is the holiest object present to your senses."

Blaise Pascal, a French mathematician, philosopher, scientist and theologian, said, "We must begin with God to properly understand man." Russian author Nikolai Berdyaev wrote, "Where there is no God, there is no man." Our goal is to look as carefully as we can at this special, crucial God-wrought creature called "man".

## I. The Sequence of Man's Creation

Think first of the *sequence* of man's creation. There is a sequence to the things that are created and the times of their creation in Genesis one. There is an ascending progression in the stated order of creation. The fact that man was created *last* was a virtual proclamation of his greatness. Man is God's highest signature, the apex of God's creation.

## II. The Seriousness of Man's Creation

Consider, secondly, the *seriousness* of man's creation. Weigh the exact words of the creation account carefully: "And God said, 'Let us make man in our image, after our likeness.'" Note that plural pronouns are used three times in that brief sentence, and that each time they are expressions by God Himself. He calls Himself *"us"*! This is not editorial license, or fanciful expression, or mere emphatic speech. This is a theology of God that emerges while He is speaking about the creation of man. This is a reflection of the Trinitarian (the One-in-three, Three-in-One) nature of God. The totality of God the Father, and God the Son, and God the Holy Spirit, was fully involved in man's creation.

This text actually tells us that the creation of man was preceded by a solemn Divine consultation! The august Persons in the Godhead met in conference to determine the dimensions of man's creation. Man was the product of a special deliberation within the Trinity, the Godhead, the Triunity of God (as if a Summit Conference between prevailing powers was being held). There is no other description like it elsewhere in the Genesis account of creation. Previously, the text said, "Let there be." Here, "let us make...." This is the language of forethought. The previous creations in Genesis one were without premeditation. Then, this is the language of resolution and determination. God speaks in order to create, but He also speaks to forever establish the truth about man. And this language expresses satisfaction. The poetic African-American poet and preacher, James Weldon Johnson, who lived in slavery days, said, "God held a parliamentary vote inside of His self, and decided to make man. Then, God reared back and 'passed a miracle'. When He was done, He sat back in satisfaction." This Divine conference alone indicates that man was to be special, unique, and different from all other earthly creatures.

## III. The Substance of the One Created

Consider the *substance* (or essence) of the one created. In verse 26, God said, "Let us make man in our image, after our likeness." Verse 27 adds, "So God created man in his own image, in the image of God created he him." Theology uses the Latin term, Imago Dei. Man was made in the image of God, after His likeness. This means that we possess in measure something that God possesses in fullness. So man the human was made to bear the image of the eternal God.

Let me draw an analogy which hopefully will help us to comprehend this "image of God" in which man is made. Suppose I hold a minted coin in my hand, a United States quarter of a dollar. It has upon one of its surfaces an image of George Washington. But George himself, the "father of our country", is not present when I hold his picture in my hand. You see, the presence of the "original" is not required in this case to reveal his image. The image is rather flat and limited, but it is there. If I leave that coin in a crack at the top of the world's tallest building, it will still bear the image. If I put it in a FedEx envelope and send it to Ambatondrazaka,

Madagascar, it will still bear the image. This is a rather crude illustration of the way every human being is made in the image of God. The relational Presence of the Great Original is not required for man's nature to be intact. The image of God conveyed by a lost man may be a thoroughgoing misrepresentation, flat and limited (and even very corrupted), but the image is still there, as distorted as it may be.

Suppose I have in my hand a small mirror and hold it before my face. My face is clearly reflected on the surface of the mirror, whether it be ugly, beautiful, or somewhere in the middle. As an aside, I learned that Woodrow Wilson, President of the United States of many years ago, often presented a favorite verse which said;

> *"For beauty I won't win a prize,*
> *Others are more handsome by far,*
> *But my face, I don't mind it, because I'm behind it,*
> *The fellow in front gets the jar."*

My image is reflected on the surface of the mirror. How long will the reflection be cast? As long as I hold the mirror before my face—and my face remains before the mirror. In this case, the presence of the "original" is required for the continuation of the reflection. This is a rather crude illustration of the manner in which a saved person "contains" and may reflect the image of God. When a sinner is saved, Jesus Christ, who is "the image of the invisible God" (Colossians 1:15), "the express image of God's Person" (Hebrews 1:3), comes into that person. The entire Christian life thereafter is a relational development between Jesus and the saved sinner. The Presence of the Original remains without interruption in the believer, and thus the Christian has at all times the potential to "continue to reflect like a mirror the splendor of the Lord" (II Corinthians 3:18, Williams translation).

As we proceed to examine this "image of God" in man, note in each case what human depravity has done in distorting and/or perverting the image. Ralph Waldo Emerson wrote of man beautifully made by God, but badly marred by guilt: "Every man is a kind of divinity in disguise. A god playing a fool. It sometimes seems as if our world is an asylum full of insane angels. Occasionally they break into their native music, and utter at intervals the words that reveal their original creation—then the mad fit leaps out of them and they mope and wallow like dogs."

In an old episode of the "All in the Family" television series, Archie Bunker disdainfully said to "Meathead", his son-in-law, "Don't you know that I am made in the image of God?" Meathead asked, *"Do you mean to say that God looks like you?"* Archie replied wryly, *"Well, I wouldn't go so far as to say that you can't tell us apart."* Aware of this puzzle in man, the enigma of Deity mixed with dirt in each case, we will examine seven characteristics of God that are parts of God's image in man:

First, man, like God, has *personality*. He, like God, is a center of self-consciousness. He, like God, has unique individuality. He is distinctive among all living creatures. He is a person, and like God, he is a spiritual Person. In John 4:24, Jesus said, "God is spirit." God is definitively spirit, but man is definitely spirit, though not spirit only. So man, like God, is a person, a spiritual person. Man is constitutionally and fundamentally a God-conscious being—man is *capax Dei*, "capable of God." One of the philosophers said, "Man is incurably religious." This is a natural expression of his spiritual personality, one feature of his likeness to God. God called other creatures into existence by His word, but man He inspired with His own breath, and so gave him a portion of His own Divine

Life. So man, too, is theopneustos—God-breathed, though unlike the Bible, he is not invested with infallibility!

One other item must be mentioned in this "God-capacity" of man—the possibility of redemption after man had sinned is as great a mark as any of the image of God impressed upon him. It was because His own image had been impressed on man that God undertook to redeem him. Man as God's mirror might have become dim, dark, distorted, broken, yet still a mirror (though marred) of the character and mind of God. Indeed, it was because that Image, though defaced, had not been totally destroyed, that the Divine redemption of man was/is possible.

When I was fourteen years of age, my family bought a home in the very center of the town where we lived. The house we moved into was located only about a hundred yards from a railroad track. Our house faced east, and the track ran north and south, so the track was behind our house. Also, the railroad track was cut down into a deep gorge, most of it cut out by man. Thus, we could not see the train, but we knew by the trembling of the earth, the rattling of our windows, and the sound of whistle and engine when a train was passing. An east-west street just a few steps from our house passed over a bridge that spanned the railroad gorge. Several times, a few friends went with me down to the track and placed coins—pennies, nickels, dimes—on the track when we heard a train approaching. Then, we would go down when the train was gone and retrieve the flattened coin. Usually, it was completely defaced and flattened into thinness. But anyone who picked it up could easily guess that it had been a penny, or a nickel, or a dime. It was still somewhat recognizable, though badly defaced. So it is with man—though fallen and "flattened", he still shows one degree or another of the original image in which he was made.

Man is like skillfully and purposely manufactured paper. Its water mark, or hallmark, is in its very texture by creation, thus, it is natural. The "later alien writing" is imposed upon the paper, thus, it is unnatural. This is the reason man is fulfilled when he finds and honors true righteousness, but he has a vagrant, pressing, uneasy (and often very hateful) spirit when he does not. Innocence and purity were original and natural to man, but sin is imposed and unnatural.

Years ago, archaeologists in old Babylon found a brick in an archaeological "dig", a brick which was stamped with the king's image — but it had been trodden on by a dog's paw while the brick was still soft and pliable, leaving the footprints of the dog superimposed over the image of the king. This is a picture of "modern" man.

One of the greatest names in the history of Christian missions is that of John G. Paton, Scottish missionary to the Hebrides Islands. When Paton went to the Hebrides Islands to minister to the fierce cannibals there, he wrote that "the natives bear the brand of savagery even upon their faces." However, his long ministry proved that this savage countenance was only a *palimpsest* scrawled by the Devil over a manuscript of the Divine finger. When the grace of God imposed its "pull" upon the hearts of the nationals in the Hebrides, the imposed writing began to be replaced by the recreation and re-emergence of the original image, the *image of God*. When Paton died, his body was buried in a burial ground in the Hebrides Islands. The nationals themselves selected his tombstone and its epitaph. It read simply,

> *"When he came, there was no light.*
> *When he died, there was no darkness."*

Because of this gracious redemption, man can know God, respond to Him, commune with Him, & cooperate with Him. Man who does not will never be or feel truly fulfilled. Having logged plenty of time and effort on both sides of the dividing line between not knowing God and knowing God in a close-up, relational way, I can testify that the difference between the two is real and radical.

Also, it is this personhood of man, modeled after God's *social* *"image"* (as a Trinity), which permits the relational and social aspects of man's nature. Remember the two names of God which are used in Genesis one and two. "Elohim" (usually translated "God") is the name that reveals His power, His creativity. "Yahweh" (usually translated "Lord") is recognized as His covenant name. This Name shows God in league, in contract, with His people.

Compare Jesus' words in Matthew 22:38-40, the two greatest commandments, both relational—one having to do with vertical relationships and one with horizontal relationships. Compare also the two great questions of God to man in Genesis 3 and 4. The first was, "Adam, where are you?" a question that reflects the vertical relation. This is not essentially a locational question, but *relational*. The second question was, "Where is your brother?" a question that reflects the *horizontal* relation.

Also, the faculty of speech (the primary means of communication between human beings) is likely a part of the image of God in man, also. "God speaks", "God says" and "the Lord says" are expressions used many, many times in the Bible.

The second mark in man that reveals the image of God in him is *purity* and the awareness of purity. The Bible consistently teaches that God is "holy", that is, that He is unique in moral character and moral commitment. God is morally separate and distinct from all other created beings. Theology says that He is "wholly Other". The Puritans spoke of Him as the "Thrice-holy God". Appended to all true holiness is the conviction of responsibility and accountability. To see how distinctive this is in God, compare (or contrast) man and God. In all the world of creaturehood, the distinction between "right" and "wrong" belongs to man alone, and is entrenched in man through the Moral Monitor called "conscience". An animal may be taught that it is not to do certain things, and it may show a semblance of conscience, but it is usually because these things are contrary to its master's wish, not because they are morally "wrong" in the intelligence of the creature.

The third mark of the image of God in man is the capacity for *perception*. Man, like God, is capable of abstract thought. Man is a rational, intelligent being. Look at I Corinthians 1-4, where Paul highlights "the wisdom of God", using the classic Greek idea of God's mind, or God's intellect. Compare the animals; they have instinct and seem to have intuition, but not rational thought. No animal approximates the intelligence of man. Compare Genesis 2:20, which says that "Adam gave names to all cattle, & to the fowl of the air, and to every beast of the field." Man studies the animals, the animals do not study man. There is no *Anthropology 101* at Animal University. Professor Huxley, a leading proponent of evolution, conceded that "there is an enormous gulf, a divergence practically infinite, between the lowest man and the highest beast." A part of that "gulf" is the perception, the intelligence, the wisdom, the discrimination, of the two. The man is highly advanced in perception, the animal is not.

Look at just one example. Consider self-consciousness, the basic, amoral concept of ego. The Greek word, *idiotes* (the Greek root is *id*, and the English derivative is the word "idiot"), which means "a fully private person." A sinner is by nature a self-curled, self-centered, self-advancing person. When his private purposing reaches total dominance, without consideration of anyone else, either God or man, he may become an *idiot*.

Both God and man are marked by self-consciousness. All three Persons of the Trinity refer in Scripture to themselves by the word "ego," or "I." Man's use of the word "I" is on demonstration every time he opens his mouth. In both persons, the mind can be voluntarily turned back in reflection on self; the person can apprehend and analyze himself, and can speak of himself as "ego," or "I", the universally recognized word for self-conscious personality. This consciousness of self is an attribute of personality which constitutes a difference, not in degree, but in kind, between the human and the merely animal. No brute has this power or capability; thus, no brute, however elevated in the scale of physical development, can properly be spoken of as a "person." That is, the sanctity that surrounds true personality cannot be attached to any animal.

Both God and man are marked by the possibility of fulfilled *purpose*, another evidence of the image of God in man. With God, this purpose is referred to as "His will" (see Ephesians 1:1-14). God wills, plans, and executes His plans. Man, too, has (derived, assigned) purpose:

*(1) To be in relationship with God;*
*(2) To represent (reflect) God.*
*(3) To rule over creation with responsible dominion.*

*(4) Redeemed man also has the charge to relay the message of redemption to those not yet redeemed.*

Another sign of the image of God in man is man's capacity for feeling and suffering. Man, like God, is capable of *passion* of personality. God is emotional in nature, but only with a perfect passion. His passion never violates His moral character or His moral commitment. Both God and man may extravagantly love and hate. The difference between God and man at this point is that God is always balanced, perfect and just in His love and hatred, while man is subject to his own fleshly frailties. Hebrews 1:9 says of Jesus, "You have loved righteousness and hated iniquity, therefore God has anointed you with the oil of gladness above your fellows." Though animals may clearly express anger and pleasure, they do not have passion such as that of man.

Another token of the image of God in man is that both may exercise *power*. Again, man's "power" and exercise of it is vastly different from God's. God's power is revealed in both His Name and His works. In Hebrew, the name *Elohim*, one of the most common words for God, emphasizes His power. The plural form is often called "the plural of power". The word could be loosely translated, "the Omni-capable, Omni-competent, Omnipotent God."

With regard to His works, God's power is manifest everywhere. Think of the power exerted by God in the original creation of all things. "By the word of His power the heavens were made," as well as all other created things. Furthermore, the universe is sustained moment-by-moment, by the same "word of His power." Man, also, is daily dependent upon God's power for all things that pertain to his existence. What a mighty God we serve!

Man, in turn, variously reflects the power that is latent in him as part of the Imago Dei. It is probably seen in man primarily as potential, though in many instances, "power" in varying expressions may easily be evidenced in individual human beings.

A tourist was standing at the railing overlooking Niagara Falls. In awe of the display of force viewed in the cascading, foaming water, he exclaimed, "That has to be the greatest unused power in the world." A Christian standing nearby quietly answered, "No, the greatest unused power in the world is the potential God stored in each of us."

A very wealthy man had an appointment in the home of a business associate. Caught in a busy schedule, he left an outing on the golf course too late to change into more suitable attire. He called on his cell phone and got clearance to come "as he was". He wore the same casual, unkempt clothes he had worn on the golf course that day. When he arrived, the family was finishing supper. The five-year-old son came out of the dining room. Seeing the guest, he said, "My Daddy says you're a millionaire. Is that right?" "Yes," the guest replied. "He says you're a self-made man. Is that right?" "I suppose you could say that." The boy looked him over carefully and then asked, "What did you make yourself like that for?" What if God said at your Final Exam, "I invested plenty of materials in you, and gave you the Perfect Plan for development and fulfillment. What did you make yourself like that for?"

It could be said of each person in his early life, "He/she has so much potential." At that point, it would be a statement of possibility and expectation. Dear friend, this is what God sees in you and says of you! But, if it is said again when you are, say, thirty years of age, it is a statement of depreciating expectancy and growing disappointment. If it is said of you at forty-five or fifty years of age, you should get away from everybody, go into a quiet place—and weep. You see, potential is your undeveloped, untapped capacity. Potential is the possibility for greatness for anyone who will follow God's exact strategy for his life. Potential is a vision of what we could be, but there must be a shift from where we only have potential to where we are actually potent, or powerful, for Him. Someone said, "Often, lost potential is the result of lack of investment. Our responsibility is not only for our own potential, but also to develop the potential of others."

I am personally convinced that the greatest sin of Christians is the sin of unfulfilled potential. If each of us knew what massive stores of potential God built into every human being, and how little it is developed and deployed for His purposes, we would be absolutely startled by the discrepancy, the vast chasm between potential and performance—between responsibility and reality. For most of us, all that treasure of potential will be nailed up with our bodies in a coffin and deposited in a grave—almost totally wasted! In a poem entitled, "The Voiceless", Oliver Wendell Holmes wrote this line: "The saddest people who ever lived are the people who die with all their music still in them." God has great power, and He has deposited it in man as potential, thus inviting (as usual) man's cooperation in its development and deployment for His glory.

Another "likeness" of God in man is the capability of *productivity*. Think of "the Word of God" of Genesis 1—the Logic of God communicated through creation. Then, think of "the Word of God" of John 1—when the Logic of God was communicated thru the Person of Christ (see Colossians 2:3), when "a Perfect human being was *God's Perfect Language*."

Then, think of "the Word of God," the Bible, which has been described as "God-in-print, speaking and acting" (See Hebrews 4:12, Isaiah 55:11). Each of these "Words" demonstrates the power and productivity of God.

Look at the "reflection" in man. Gen 2:2 calls creation "God's work": "And the seventh day God ended His work, which He had made" (twice in one verse). Then, in the Ten Commandments (Exodus 20), the same word is used for man's work: (20:9) "Six days you shall labor, and do all of your work."

Man is again like God in that he is a (modified) creator. I stood recently with a new father, who was proudly holding in his arms his new-born son. I said, "How does it feel to know that you joined God in an act of creation?" He happily replied, "Herb, it's the greatest thing I've ever done!"

Works of art are often called the artist's "creations." One philosopher said, "Just as God has His universe, in which are mirrored the eternal, archetypal Ideas of the Divine Mind, so human civilization is Man's 'universe', the aggregate product of his intelligence and creative activity." As usual, man's creative works are marred by his flesh, his frailty, and the faultiness of his sins, but they are still demonstrations of remarkable productivity.

An astounding statement is made in Ephesians 2:10 in your New Testament. "We are God's workmanship," the text says (King James Version). The Greek word translated "workmanship" is *"poiema"*, from which we derive our English word, "poem". The word is used twice in the New Testament, once in Ephesians 2:10, the other in Romans 1:20. The Romans passage provides incredible insights into the idea of God's power and productivity. It says (Amplified Bible), "Ever since the creation of the world God's invisible nature and attributes, that is, His eternal power and Divinity, have been made intelligible and clearly discernible in and through the things that have been made (His handiworks)." The term, "the things that have been made (His handiworks)" is an attempt to translate the single Greek word, "poiema." So both man and material creation are described in the New Testament as "God's poems"! What is a poem? It is a designed, rhythmic creation, fashioned to exhibit the mind of the creator and to communicate that mind to any "reader" or observer. In both of its New Testament occurrences, the "poem" is a product of the Ultimate Mind, a thing made, a piece of workmanship, a "work of art", a "masterpiece." The last two expressions have often been used to translate the Greek word.

Some years ago, on a trip to Brazil, I checked Ephesians 2:10 in a Portuguese Bible, and made a great discovery. The Portuguese translation of "His workmanship" was *"sua feitura,"* which means *"His (God's) feature attraction."* Man is God's feature attraction, and redeemed man is God's "Headline" to display Himself to the rest of men who remain unredeemed. Man is the ultimate product of God's mighty creative wisdom and power, and there are faint echoes still remaining in fallen man of that creative wisdom and power. Remember: this is the very first aspect under which God is presented to us in Scripture: "In the beginning, God created..." Today, the man in Christ should be a modified demonstration of God's continuing wisdom and creativity.

Here is the "bottom-line" of this point: man was made in the "similitude" of God, and man is to show that resemblance with which he has been endowed by creation. Fallen man still reflects the dim image of

God, but new men in Christ are to be much clearer finite expressions of the Infinite God (see Ephesians 4, Romans 8:29).

## IV. The Splendor of His Character

It must not be forgotten that man (we) were made to Relate, to Represent, and to Rule (note the order). We were made for *relationships* — with God, with ourselves, with each other, with creation, etc. Then, we were made to be a *re-presentation* of God to the universe. It has been said that the Old Testament is the *audio* phase of God's revelation, the New Testament is the *video* phase, and each Christian is to be "an *audio-visual replay*". Then, we were made to *rule*. That is, we were made to "have dominion over all of creation." One of the great verses of the Bible is Romans 5:17, which reads (Amplified Bible), "If because of one man's trespass (lapse, offense) death reigned through that one, much more surely will those who receive (God's) overflowing grace and the free gift of righteousness (putting them into right standing with Himself) reign as kings in life through the one Man Jesus Christ." Here, the splendor of man is seen at its highest. Let the "dedication line" of the Book of Revelation be the conclusion to this chapter. "Unto Him who loves us, and loosed us from our sins in His own blood, and has made us kings and priests unto God and His Father; to Him be glory and dominion forever and ever" (Revelation 1:5-6). "Man is one entire world, & he has been placed in another entire world so he could rule it and it could resource him." Man is God's highest achievement, and in him He has made a living revelation of Himself.

The one thing that upstages everything else in chapter two of the Book of Genesis is the Construction of a MATE for Adam, and the Commencement of MARRIAGE. We will deal with that in the next chapter.

*Chapter 3*

# THE MARRIAGE AND MATING OF MAN

*"And the LORD God said, 'It is not good that the man should be alone; I will make him an help meet for him.' And out of the ground the LORD God formed every beast of the field, and every fowl of the air; and brought them unto Adam to see what he would call them: and whatsoever Adam called every living creature, that was the name thereof. And Adam gave names to all cattle, and to the fowl of the air, and to every beast of the field; but for Adam there was not found an help meet for him. And the LORD God caused a deep sleep to fall upon Adam, and he slept: and he took one of his ribs, and closed up the flesh instead thereof; And the rib, which the LORD God had taken from man made he a woman, and brought her unto the man. And Adam said, This is now bone of my bones, and flesh of my flesh: she shall be called Woman, because she was taken out of Man. Therefore shall a man leave his father and his mother, and shall cleave unto his wife: and they shall be one flesh."* **(Genesis 2:18-24)**

A teacher was reading to her elementary class the story of Cinderella. She ran out of time in the final chapter and simply abbreviated the ending. She said, "Then the handsome prince and the beautiful princess lived happily ever after." One little boy in the class blurted out innocently, "Oh, no, they didn't; they got married!" Another child in a history class was telling the story of Patrick Henry. He said, "Patrick Henry got married, and then he said, 'Give me liberty or give me death!'" another, telling the story of Benjamin Franklin, reported, "Then Benjamin Franklin moved to Philadelphia, got married, and discovered electricity!"

Marriage was man's first social institution, preceding the state, the school and the church. How God provided for marriage and the home is recorded in Genesis chapters one and two.

## I. The Provision for the Mate and the Marriage

*God's provisions for a mate for Adam and a marriage between Adam and Eve* are stated in Genesis 2:18. In one verse, God informs us of several important realities in understanding God's domestic design for man.

Note, first, that both the mate for Adam and the marriage of Adam and his mate were made in a setting of *Divine Providence*. Verses 16, 17, and 18 begin with the phrase, "And the Lord God...." Thus, there is a succession of very significant declarations from God in these verses. Each of the declarations contains a requirement or an assignment from God. The first (verse 15) concerns the placement of Adam in the Garden with an assignment to "dress it and to keep it." The second significant declaration from God (verses 16 and 17) contains both a permission and a prohibition. The permission was, "Of every tree of the Garden you may freely eat." The prohibition was, "But of the tree of the knowledge of good and evil, you shall not eat of it." Incidentally, the "you" in Genesis 2:17 is singular in the Hebrew, referring only to Adam, but later, it changes to a plural, including Eve. So the man was the responsible party, and Adam is constantly shown in Scripture to be the representative of the human race in the Garden of Eden. And the penalty for violating the prohibition was clearly and decisively stated, "For in the day you eat thereof you shall surely die." The third significant declaration of God (verse 18) was, "It is not good that the man should be alone; I will make an help meet ('a companion suitable') for him." So God sovereignly presided over everything that happened here. Divine Providence initiated the construction of a mate for Adam and the marriage of Adam and Eve.

Marriage and the home were both created by God, forming the basic foundational unit for society and human relationships. The institution of marriage, the foundation for the home, was generated out of the creative goodwill of God toward man. The origination of the institution of marriage and the home is, in turn, the foundation for a *Christian* marriage and a *Christian* home. So both of them are "good" in Heaven's best sense. Each has the possibility of "Heaven on earth" inherent in it. What confidence and reassurance this should breed as a Christian couple approach their marriage. If they desire God's perfect will and play by His regulations, they may be sure of God's control and blessing in their marriage.

Note, second, that both the mate for Adam and the marriage between them were made against the background of a *deep problem*. Verse 18b says (and note again that the initiative belonged to God), "And the LORD God said, It is not good that the man should be alone; I will make him a companion suitable to him."

After a long lineup of declarations in which God said about His creation, "It was good" (Genesis 1:4, 10, 12, 18, 21, 25, 31), there comes the only malediction ("not good") in Genesis 2:18. With all the superlative benedictions, there was one sad malediction. "It is not good that the man should be alone." One writer said that "before Adam was fully aware of his incompleteness without a wife, God anticipated his need and planned to meet it. Adam's wife was in the mind of God long before she was ever in the arms of Adam."

Genesis 2:20 says, "But for Adam there was not found a companion suitable for him." With all of the new species of life God created, Adam apparently hoped he would find one fit to be his own companion, one with physical, mental and spiritual equipment to match his. But with the appearance of each new creature, the man knew he was a different order from each and all of the animal world. He was linked with them, but distinct from them. He was more than animal, but less than God—so he was all alone. On the one hand, Jehovah Elohim ("the LORD God") was too high, while all the other creatures were too low, for such a partnership as Adam's nature required and craved. And so Adam dwelt in solitude apart from both. Note this carefully: Adam was nobly created, but essentially alone.

God made man to be a social creature, and there was no one else present in the Garden with whom personal relationship could be established. One comic said, "The only thing God ever made which He pronounced 'not good' was a bachelor." Another comic replied, "But have you considered the bonus—no mothers-in-law, either!" One distant friend wrote to another, "My mother-in-law is at the gate of death; would you please come and help pull her through?" I record this humor freely because my mother-in-law was one of the kindest, godliest, sweetest Christian women I have ever known (and my wife is cut from the same cloth; I feel that I am blessed with even more "good" than Adam had!!!). When God finally presented Eve to Adam, fresh from His creative Hand,

Adam exclaimed (according to one translation), "Now, at last!" Another free translation records it, "Now You're cookin'!"

Note, thirdly, that God's provision to solve the problem of personal loneliness was based on a statement of *decisive Divine purpose*, and was followed by an act that fulfilled that purpose. In verse 18c, God said, "I will make him a companion suitable for him."

## II. The Preparation of the Mate for the Marriage

In verses 19-22, we see *the preparation of the mates for the marriage*. God wisely prepared each of the mates for their coming marriage. He took great pains to get each ready for the other and for the relationship.

In verses 19-20, we are first informed of *the preparation of Adam for Eve*. This preparation was basically psychological preparation. Adam's first lesson was to learn to appreciate his wife, and this remains a first lesson for any husband in a marriage today.

Adam's "animal assignment", or his project to name the animals, is stated in these words, "And God brought them unto Adam, to see what he would call them." This assignment emphasized to Adam that, though he could exercise rulership over the animals, he could not have fellowship with them. There was not one among them qualified to be a suitable companion for him (verse 20b). Through this sense of deprivation Adam was prepared for God's creation of Eve as that companion.

Then, in verses 21-24, we see *the preparation of Eve for Adam*. Eve's construction was both physical and psychological—that is, God made another human being with a healthy body, a happy soul, and a holy spirit. Eve was, like Adam, indwelt by God and thus a ready companion for Adam. Additionally, both Adam and Eve had representative and symbolic significance, he as "the first Adam", anticipating a "last Adam", and she the bride of Adam taken from his side ("out of the wound came the wife"), anticipating the Church, the Bride of Christ taken from His wounded side.

It is significant that verse 21 says that "God caused a deep sleep to fall upon Adam, and he slept." For Adam, there was no frantic running after a wife. There was no sulking because he didn't have one. He simply "went to sleep in the will of God," and waited. There was no "dear hunting" in the Garden of Eden! At this point, their confidence in God was implicit and rich; they did not have to worry about self-sponsorship. While Adam was asleep, God "took one of his ribs, and closed up the flesh instead thereof," and out of this part of Adam, God constructed Eve. Thus, they had a natural affinity for each other. An affinity is a match that two things have for each other, as a baseball and a baseball bat, or a basketball and the goal that it passes through, or an electrical plug and the wall socket into which it fits. Male and female have an affinity for each other, designed of God. Any other kind of relationship for either of them is a violation of their natures, a violation of the natural order, and a violation of the will of God.

Verse 22 says that God removed a side of Adam's nature and "made" a woman. The word is an engineering term—God "constructed" a woman out of the man—and "He brought her to the man" (playing the roles of the minister and the best man in a modern marriage ceremony). Thus, the stage was set for them to enjoy each other in God's institution of marriage.

## III. The Purposes of the Mate and the Marriage

Because so many of these truths are presented throughout the message, let me only briefly mention here the *purposes of the mate(s) and the marriage.*

The first purpose was *companionship with/for each other.* Previously, Adam was "alone" (2:18). Now, he was companioned by one suitable to him. The companionship was to be mutually enjoyable and mutually responsible.

The second purpose was that each was to find *completeness* in the other. Neither was to be a competer in the relationship, but each was to be a completer of the other. An alternate translation of the Old Testament translates the word "rib" by the words "flank" or "side", suggesting the understanding that without woman, a gap was left in Adam's nature, a side of his nature was missing.

The third purpose of the relationship was *cooperation* and *contribution.* A note of explanation: though I am speaking primarily of Eve because she was the one created purposefully from Adam, these are mutual realities which apply to each person in the relationship. The term "help meet" or "helpmate" suggests a fellow-worker (not a beast of burden, not a slave, not a piece of property*).*

The fourth purpose was the *communion* of body, soul and spirit. The total person, including the physical, the mental and psychological complex of mind, emotions and will, and the spiritually developing lives of the two, are to be blended into one in the marital vocation.

The fifth purpose is that of *creation,* or procreation "after their kind" (but again, the woman is not a mere outlet for the male sexual expression, nor a mere 'baby factory'). Note the implication of the word "fruitful" in Genesis 1:28. This is not an accidental use of the word; it is advisable, so that we may understand that God's purpose for human beings, both physically and spiritually, is that they may multiply as any single unit of fruit may do, and the implication that each piece of fruit has infinite potential for future multiplication must not be ignored spiritually. Else why would God refer to children as "fruit"? According to the Book of Acts, multiplication is the intended outcome of proper spiritual ministry. Years ago, Daniel Mazia, the head of the UCLA science department, said, "Any species that does not multiply will die." This is especially true in spiritual ministry, where we minister in a world with a population that is exploding through multiplication. Furthermore, we must be careful to distinguish between replication or duplication and multiplication. Multiplication is an ever-enlarging future product, but that must be guaranteed by the transfer of the concept into and through each new believer and then necessarily into and through each of his disciples, "the men God gives to him." When the disciple-making process is practiced accurately and adequately as mandated and modeled in the New Testament, multiplication will occur.

The sixth purpose is for *community*. There was to be a common unity in all marriages, and the extended result was to be social community, enlarging and earth-filling.

The seventh purpose of the marriage and mating of man and woman was for the *communication* of a crucial message. Their union was to model and to manifest the relation of Christ the Bridegroom and His Bride, the Church. The "marriage message" is to be delivered "live" by every Christian family; i.e., modeled among men.

## IV. The Personal Role of the Mate

Fourth, note the *personal role* of Eve, Adam's mate, in the story. Note, too, the ascending scale of importance in the list. What was Eve to be to Adam?

First, she was to be a *counterpart* to him, and thus they were to be a match for each other. Eve's distinctiveness as a female matched and suited Adam's distinctiveness as a male. God established the affinity of man for woman and woman for man when He created Adam and engineered Eve from Adam's body, but they then had to play out daily the role of matching and meshing with each other. No such engineered affinity exists in any relationship in a marriage other than male and female.

Second, she was to be a *completement* (a *complement*) to Adam, a part of his being and nature without which he could not be complete. There is a subtle indication of this in the text of Scripture. Until the creation of woman, the word for "man" was *adam*, which means "man" or "mankind". Adam was the personification of man or mankind. But when woman was created, the word for man became *ish*, which means "male" in contradistinction to *ishah*, "female." Man did not distinctively become male until there was female, and there is a "side" to man that is missing when he is without her.

Let me tell a story about this "side" that God removed from Adam to make Eve. A mother was reading and explaining to her young son the story of the construction of Eve out of the side of Adam. Later that same afternoon, she found the boy on the couch in the living room, moaning and holding his side. When she asked if his side was hurting, he replied, "Yes! I think I'm having a wife!"

Third, Eve was to be the *correspondent* to Adam. Thus, a mutual co-respondence, a mutual "give and take", was to be established as a day-to-day function of their lives together. He was to respond to her lovingly, and she was to respond to him submissively. Question: would a wife not tend to submit readily to a husband who loves her "as Christ loved the church (*agape* love—self-sacrificing, self-disinterested, self-giving), and gave Himself for it?" And would not such a loving husband want to perfectly care for a wife who submits like that? So their marriage would be a holy "competition" of loving and submitting. They would love each other mutually, initiated by the love of the husband, and they would submit themselves to each other mutually (Ephesians 5:21), initiated by the submission of the wife to her husband. There would be a *co*-respondence of each to the other.

Fourth, Eve was to be the *companion* of Adam. I mention this without further comment here, because it is considered elsewhere in this study.

Fifth, Eve was to be a *co-creator* with Adam. Again, I mention this only briefly here. Though pro-creation is not the sole purpose of the marriage of a husband and a wife, as some erroneously say it is, it is nonetheless a very important reason for the relationship. One of my friends said at the time of his marriage to a precious Christian lady, "For the first few years, we hope to 'make some babies'," and he was simply expressing one of the main purposes of marriage.

My wife and I were visiting one day in the home of precious Christian friends. The son in the family had married quite some time before, and he and his wife had just had their first child. It was obvious when I saw him that he was "bustin' his buttons" with appreciation, amazement and pride. I asked happily, "Well, how is it to be a Daddy?" He replied, "Herb, I've never been involved in anything like it!" I said, "Isn't it amazing to lean over the cradle of your own newborn son and feel that you helped God create something?" He answered with quiet pride, "Yes, and I've never made anything before like that little boy!"

Sixth, Eve was to stand alongside of her husband as a fellow *community-builder*. It was obvious from the beginning that their children were to be the first generation in a multiplication process that was to "fill the earth," and thus they were to be significant parts of an earthly community of human beings, a society of people, and were to live with a cosmopolitan ("world citizen") view of their lives. Though this has been tragically missed by most Christians today, this is still God's intention for each Christian couple, for their families, and for their world-involvement in the cause of Christ. He intends today to use each Christian (far, far more than the typical Christian seems to know) to build a vast world-wide community (common unity) of believers in Christ, always enlarging and expanding through the strategy and action of the cosmopolitan Christian. I insist that this "strategy and action" are the responsibilities of the individual Christian (though, of course, he will work with others in the fellowship of believers—but his responsibility cannot be fulfilled merely by cooperative effort with others), and I refuse to say that this "strategy and action" are primarily the responsibility of the local church. I think this is what has produced the imbalance of international impact in the Christian community which has left the western world over-saturated and *weak* (and getting weaker by the hour). According to the New Testament, each Christian life is viewed as a "marriage to Christ" (Romans 7:4), and the expectation is that it be a life of union and communion with Christ and reproduction and multiplication for Christ. Just as Adam and Eve were united under a command to "be fruitful and multiply, and fill the earth," the same assignment is to be spiritually fulfilled by each Christian through his/her union with Christ and his/her obedience to His intent and command. In any species, reproduction takes place one-and-one, not in mass!

While I am "in the neighborhood", let me add that all Christians fall into one of two categories—they are either provincial, parochial Christians or cosmopolitan, world-citizen Christians. Because the typical church doesn't seem to give too much attention to the distinction, both of these Christians "travel incognito" (one woman misstated her anonymity by saying, 'I'm traveling in embryo') in large numbers in today's church.

Provincial Christians are very narrow in focus, restricted, confined and small-minded. In that sense, though they may appear to be happy, celebrating, worshipping, faithful Christians, their horizon is bounded by their little world. Their *horizon* does not match God's *heart*. Their philosophy is unwittingly "us four (or whatever number that constitutes their local involvement in the church), and no more." They would be shocked to know that the New Testament thinks they are *petty*, and that they are missing the "big thing" God has in mind for each of His children. They will be shocked, also, to finally realize that vast, vast potential for world impact and world revolution for Christ's sake and for the good of billions of people, remained stored in the box of what David Bryant called "their pea-sized Christianity". Provincial Christians are always focused on small, local, self-serving, "growth" purposes—*self*-attentiveness, *self*-survival, *self*-growth, *self*-enjoyment, and *self*-gratification, even if they have "broader" interests that spread out through a "missionary church".

That sounds good, but it is far, far short of Christ's goal for His redeemed child.

Cosmopolitan Christians, on the other hand, are easy to identify. They seem to be "stand-out saints," but they are merely New Testament Christians. Vance Havner said, "Christians today are usually so sub-normal that should they become normal, everyone would think of them as abnormal." A cosmopolitan Christian is large-hearted (his heart is truly *world*-big), big-spirited, all-embracing, non-threatened, tactful though not compromising, sensitive though not sentimental, and versatile in thought and action. He is like Atlas in that he literally carries the world on/in his heart. He is like Napoleon's soldiers, who carried a map of the world colored in the tri-colors of France in their knapsack. In this case, the Christian's world map is colored crimson-red because he can envision the whole world covered with the redeeming blood of Jesus Christ—and he carries this "map" in his heart. He has allowed God to swell his three-cornered heart until it is as big as planet earth, and he acts out in his daily life the burden of involvement and investment in the whole wide world. He is a true "ambassador for Christ," a diplomat for the Kingdom of God. Paul is the classic example of the cosmopolitan Christian, and his personal testimony in I Corinthians 9:19-22 is the classic statement of such a Christian. So you see, Christian, it is no small thing when I say that God's intention for Eve was that she stand alongside Adam as a social, cosmopolitan community-builder!

Meanwhile, back at the house! Seventh, Eve was to be a joint testimony alongside of Adam, simply by living in a marriage and a home such as God intended, by which Jesus Christ, the promised Deliverer, and His relationship with His Bride, the Church, would be *communicated* to their children, to the culture that would arise through their children, and to the world of men to the end of time.

This is the personal role to be assumed by Eve in her relationship with Adam, and by every wife in her relationship with her husband. This is why God "engineered" Eve's construction from a "side" of Adam's body.

## V. The Divine Prescription for a Biblical Marriage

Fifth and finally, we will consider the *Divine prescription* for a Biblical marriage. Genesis 2:24 says, "Therefore shall a man leave his father and his mother, and shall cleave unto his wife, and they shall be one flesh. And they were both naked, the man and his wife, and were not ashamed." This announcement probably sounded very strange to Adam, and he might have said, *"Father? Mother? What are they?"*

Here we see the prescribed conditions, three of them, for a Biblical marriage. Here is marriage according to God's original plan. What does it involve? There are three essentials prescribed in the Biblical formula. Note that in all three requirements, the man is to be the initiator. He is the one responsible to lead the couple, and he is especially responsible to consolidate his attention on his wife. Why the man? Because when a marriage fails, it is usually the man whose eye, mind and heart first stray in the relationship. Here, he is made most responsible to prevent such straying.

First, there must be a *leaving*. "A man shall leave his father and his mother." "'Tying the knot' is meant to cut off all circulation!" There can be no true marriage without this. Just as a baby can't grow up unless the umbilical cord is severed, neither can a man and woman have a successful and happy marriage unless the "unbiblical cord" of continuing attachments to all other relationships is severed. A marriage cannot grow up and develop as long as no clear separation from one's family takes place. Ideally, the connection between the child and the father's purse strings and the mother's apron strings is to be severed when the bride is given in marriage at the altar. From that moment, the couple will seek their ultimate security, emotionally as well as financially, in each other.

Someone will say, "We are taught in the Bible to love our parents, not to leave them, and now we are told that we must leave them." Yet leaving them for the sake of the marriage does not mean to totally abandon them, to become totally derelict from them, or to leave them in the lurch. It means that the consolidation of a man's or woman's attention in a marriage must be to his/her mate. In fact, only if a husband and wife are given the chance to leave and to start their own home, only if they are independent, will they be able to take responsibility for their families later on and serve them. The purse strings and apron strings that once were attached between a child and its family must be cut when the child matures and enters into marriage.

Second, there must be a *cleaving*. "A man shall leave his father and his mother, and shall cleave unto his wife." The Hebrew word used here means "to stick to," "to paste," "to be glued to." A full adherence is called for; a full attachment, a full loyalty, and remember, it is the man's responsibility to lead in maintaining this attachment.

Note the order: "leaving" precedes "cleaving." Plainly, marriage, nothing less, must come before intercourse. Leaving and cleaving belong together. Cleaving is clinging; to cleave is to cling. In an ideal marriage, the husband and wife cling to one another, not in desperation, but in the calm assurance that God wants them to face life together. Leaving describes the public and legal aspect of marriage, cleaving describes the personal and intimate aspects. You cannot truly cleave unless you first totally leave. And you should not leave unless you have fully decided to cleave.

A husband and a wife are glued together like two pieces of paper. If you try to separate the two pieces of paper which are glued together, you tear them both. If you try to separate a husband and wife who cleave together, both are hurt.

Another consequence of being glued together is that husband and wife are closer to each other than either of them can be in any other relationship, closer than to anything or anyone else in the world. Their relationship is more important than the husband's work or profession, more important than the wife's housecleaning and cooking or, in case she works, than her profession. It is more important than the husband's friends or the wife's friends, more important than visitors and guests, even more important than the children.

Cleaving means love of a special kind. It is love in which the partners have made a decision and thus it is no longer a groping, searching, seeking love, a love that awaits fulfillment. Love which cleaves is mature love, love which has decided to remain faithful—faithful to one person—and to share with this one person one's whole life.

Finally, there must be a *weaving*. "And they shall be one flesh." Note that the primary attention no longer falls on the man. It is now on both (compare Ephesians 5:21-33). Each partner in the marriage should say, "My marriage does not exist for me, but for us—and for God's glory." Here, a mutual responsibility is prescribed. "They shall be one flesh."

This also refers to the sexual intimacy of marriage, an intimacy that requires a mutual consent and cooperation.

Sex originated with God; it was His idea for ultimate relationship between a male and a female. It was not initiated in a back alley atmosphere, or by two illicit partners. Because it is God's idea, we must understand it from His perspective. We must be free to talk about it in order to understand the complexities and intimacies and exclusiveness of it. The physical union of husband and wife is as dear to and as near to God as is their faithfulness to each other and the legality and sanctity of their marriage.

We must not see this "one flesh" as merely referring to sex in marriage. To become one flesh with a mate in marriage means more than just the physical union. It means that two persons share everything they have, not only their bodies or material possessions, but also their thinking and feeling, their joy and suffering, their hopes and fears, their successes and failures. Their bodies (physical and sexual union), their souls (mental and emotional union), and their spirits (spiritual union) are woven together to create a common personhood between them. The two become completely one, and still they maintain their individual persons. Each is not a half, each is a whole person, but two whole persons make an entirely new entity or unity.

This compatibility is to be achieved, it is not automatically received. It is a goal, not a gift.

One Christian counselor gave this illustration: "I once saw three jugglers in a circus. They stood at equal distance from each other, like three points in a triangle. Each one threw objects to both of their partners and received objects from both. Each one had to give as well as to receive.

As long as they were able to keep up the rhythm of giving and receiving, the game went on in perfect harmony." Marriage is like that. It requires (and greatly rewards) the skill of giving and receiving. When such giving occurs, a gluing occurs. When such receiving occurs, a beautiful relationship emerges.

This, then, is God's original prescription for marriage, and remains God's plan for Christian marriage. This is the marriage and the mating for which man and woman were made.

One other thing needs to be firmly stated before this study is completed. In Ephesians 5:22-33, the Bible presents marriage as a symbol of the union between Christ and His Church. This goes all the way back to Genesis two, where Eve was taken from the "side" or "flank" of Adam after "the LORD God caused a deep sleep to fall upon Adam, and he slept" (Genesis 2:21). In the same manner, the Church, the Bride of Christ, was taken from the spear pierced side of Jesus when He died on the Cross. The Church is the product of the sufferings of Jesus at Calvary, and is "bone of His bone and flesh of His flesh."

After Paul had spoken of the structure of a marriage and had declared the responsibility of the wives (Ephesians 5:22-24) and of the husbands (Ephesians 5:25-31), he then referred to the symbol contained in the marriage arrangement when he said, "This is a great mystery; I speak concerning Christ and His Church." Consider our last points in this message: when a man leaves father and mother to be married—this is a great mystery. When the man cleaves to his wife, this is a great mystery. When the two become "one flesh", this is a great mystery. "I speak concerning Christ and His Church," Paul added. "I take this to be a picture, a pattern, a portrait of Christ and His Church." So true marriage is a triangle, and earthly marriage is intended to deliver a Heavenly message based on a Heavenly model.

The deepest mystery of the triangle is Jesus Christ Himself! Because He loved us, He "left" His Father at the moment of His conception in the womb of the Virgin Mary. So His part involved a "leaving". Jesus did not regard equality with God a thing to be hoarded unto Himself, but put the full expression of it aside in Heaven to become man. He "emptied Himself", He "humbled Himself and became obedient unto Death, even the Death of the Cross!"

Because He loved/loves us, He cleaves to us, fully and perfectly identifying Himself with us and us with Him. He cleaves to us tenaciously and perfectly, holding us securely in the palm of His Hand (John 10:28-30). Indeed, He makes us "members of His Body," so we are as secure as He is.

Let's admit at this point that the Church is sometimes a difficult wife. She can be self-centered and selfish. She can be disobedient. She can even try to "run the Household," telling even the Divine Bridegroom what to do! But He has patiently cleft Himself to the Church, and though she may be unfaithful to Him (like Gomer was to Hosea, another picture of the Church as the Bride and Jesus as the Bridegroom), "He remains faithful, because He cannot deny Himself" (again, like Hosea, a type of Christ, did to Gomer, a type of the Church). Jesus may have to deal roughly with "His Wife", but He will never leave her nor forsake her. He never "walks out" on His Bride, even if she deserves such abandonment! He is always ready with His forgiveness, with His kindness, with His goodwill, with His restoration. He "loved the Church and gave Himself for her" (Ephesians 5:25), then He "sanctified her, having cleansed her with the washing of water by His Word" (Ephesians 5:26). Then verse 27 says (Amplified Bible), having prepared her for the great moment, He then "presented the Church to Himself in glorious splendor, without spot (any blemish imposed from the outside) or wrinkle (any defect developed from the inside) or any such thing, that she might be holy and blameless"!!!

There is a *weaving* between Christ and His Church which will be perfected beyond the Veil of time and sense, in Heaven, where Jesus and His Church will enjoy sympathetic and perfect union *forever.* She then will be on exhibit before the universe as His Love-Trophy, His Bride, *FOREVER!* Remember, Christian husband, that when you love your wife (Ephesians 5:25), you are presenting a picture of the great Bridegroom, Jesus, to the world, and Christian wife, remember that when you submit to your husband (Ephesians 5:22), you are presenting to the world a visual representation of His Church and its relationship to Him. May God forgive us when we fail, and may He help us to allow them to see Him and His union with us through us and our domestic relationships!!

*Chapter 4*

# THE MAKEUP OF MAN

*"And the very God of peace sanctify you wholly; and I pray God your whole spirit and soul and body be preserved blameless unto the coming of our Lord Jesus Christ." 1 Thessalonians 5:23*

In the children's classic, *Alice in Wonderland*, Lewis Carroll tells of an animated padlock, running excitedly everywhere. When it was asked why the desperate search, the padlock replied, "I am looking for the key to unlock myself." Modern man seems to be on such a search, running frantically everywhere, looking for both self-understanding and self-fulfillment. Many keys may fit into the lock of man's personality, but only one will turn it and allow him to function properly. That key is provided by man's Maker, and it is presented to us in His Book, the Bible. What do we find out about ourselves in His Book?

# I. God's Design of Man

First, we discover in God's Book the account of *God's design of man*. When God made man (Genesis 1:26), he made Him "in His own image, after His likeness." We may not be able to fully detect everything that this means, but we can be certain about many things. Among other things, it means that God made man a trinity, a tri-unity, like Himself. God is Father, Son, and Holy Spirit. Man is comprised of "spirit, soul, and body" (I Thessalonians 5:23). The specified order in that verse shows the order of significance of the three "parts" of man. When God created man, He obviously created Him by plan, by design, and with clear intention as to his structure and purpose. It is clear that God Himself dwelt within man. It is equally clear that the "compartment" of man in which He dwelt was the human spirit.

The first "part" of man specified in the text is the *spirit*. The human spirit is the dwelling place of God within a man. If God dwells within man at all, He will dwell in man's spirit. At man's creation, the Holy Spirit of God dwelt unrestricted within the human spirit of man.

The second specified "part" of man by creation is the human *soul*. Man's soul is comprised of his mind, emotions, and will. These together make up man's "psychological" life. The Greek word for "soul" is *psuche*, which is the prefix of our English word, "psychology." So the soul of man is his psychological life. When God created man, it is evident that God dwelt in the highest part, or the most central part, of man's being in order to control him "inside-out." This control was intended to bring glory to God and good to man. As long as man was operated "under control" by God Himself, he was "whole."

The final specified part of man by creation is the human *body*. What a marvel the human body is! The body is a complex of intricate cells (billions of them), intricate members, and intricate connections. Truly, we are "fearfully and wonderfully made" (Psalm 139:14). The body is the vehicle for the self-expression of the person who lives in it.

Man is a tri-unity. All three "parts" of the man must maintain inter-connection and inter-communication if he is to function properly in this life. It was God's original design to control the man from his inner spirit, with the control revealed in the man's mind, emotions, and will (his soul), and that the activity of the body reveal the inner control God maintained in the spirit and soul of the man.

F. B. Meyer, the great British Christian pastor and author, wrote, "The soul, the center of our personality, can operate in two worlds. From its level we can ascend into union with the Unseen and Eternal through the spirit, or we may descend into union with the earth through the body. The soul looks out on two spheres: it is related to the invisible sphere by the spirit; it is related to the visible sphere by the body." If the spirit of man is filled with the Spirit of God, and the soul of man comes under the control of that Spirit, the man is "spiritual." If the soul of man relates only to the body and the two of them act in conjunction, the man is either "natural" (a lost man) or "carnal" (a self-centered Christian).

The functions of the three — spirit, soul, and body — are clear. The body is the means by which the individual is *world*-conscious, or conscious of his surroundings. The soul is the means by which the individual is *self*-conscious, or conscious of himself. By means of the soul, the individual is also socially conscious, or conscious of other self-conscious and socially conscious human beings like himself. By means of the spirit, the individual is *God*-conscious. The spirit of man is the organ of relationship with God. He may have an academic awareness of God by means of his soul, but he will only have relationship with God by means of his spirit. Jesus said, "God is spirit, and they that worship Him must worship Him in spirit and in truth" (John 4:24).

## II. God's Dilemma with Man

Second, we discover in God's Book that *God faces a dilemma with man*. How long man remained in the original condition in which he was created we do not know. The Bible tells us that Satan came to man in the Garden of Eden and tempted him to sin. Man of his own will chose to believe the lie by which Satan tempted him rather than the truth of God. God said, "Of every tree of the garden you may freely eat: But of the tree of the knowledge of good and evil, you shall not eat of it: for in the day that you eat thereof you shall surely die" (Genesis 2:16, 17). The Hebrew construction of the last sentence of verse 17 is very enlightening. It literally says, "In the day that you eat of it, dying, you shall die." This is an enlightening reference to two deaths which occurred in conjunction with man's sin. The word "dying" is present tense and indicates that the death would occur simultaneous with the act of sin. The term, "you shall die," is future tense, and refers to another death that would occur later. This is precisely what happened when Adam sinned. Adam died instantaneously in his spirit the moment he sinned (we will look more closely at this later), and then he died physically (that is, his body died) some time later when the effects of the spiritual death spread throughout his being with its fatal effect. Adam (and every man born of Adam) experienced a double death because of the Fall. So it is apparent that, since Adam sinned, God has a major dilemma in dealing with man.

The dilemma may be pictured by a simple illustration. Man's nature is like a three-story building. The top floor is the spirit; the middle floor is the soul; and the lower floor is the body. Beginning at the bottom, the lower story is the "basement" of the house. The middle story is the "workshop" where plans are devised, excitement is aroused, and decisions are made. The top story is the "observatory," the place of communion, meditation and relationship with God. It is this upper floor, man's spirit, his capacity for God that lifts man above every other creature in God's creation.

If the man only had the two lower floors, he would only have a "natural" life. The top floor gives man a capacity for God, the possibility of a "spiritual" life. It is the presence and proper function of the upper floor that enables man to have the very Life of God within him. In the famous parable of the Prodigal Son, the boy rejected his father, went into a "far country" both geographically and spiritually, and personally lived for a while in the lower part of the house. But he could not remain content on that level. He "came to himself" and arose and went to his father (both geographically and spiritually), thus moving back into the top floor of human experience. The upper floor must be occupied by God and fully functional in the way God intended in order for man to be truly human.

This illustration of man as a three-story house will help us to see what happened when Adam sinned. We call this terrible event "the Fall of man." To follow the illustration, when Adam sinned, it was as if a giant bomber flew over the house and dropped a deadly bomb squarely on the top floor. The bomb obliterated the top floor, blowing it away. The second floor also received the devastating effects of the blast. It was badly damaged and deteriorated. And the effects reached the bottom floor also, causing damage that would at last destroy that floor, too. So the Fall of man was like "The Fall of the House of Usher." A great collapse took place when Adam sinned, in which the spirit (the upper floor in the illustration) died instantly, the soul (the middle floor) was badly damaged and died progressively, and the body (the lower floor) received the effects of the downward drain of death so that it died ultimately.

The word "Fall" aptly describes the result of Adam's sin. In the instant that he sinned, he fell into a life that was sub-human, more animal than man. He is called "the natural man" in I Corinthians 2:14. That is, he was suddenly without the normal supernatural frame of reference with which he was created. He had lost God, and thus he had no inner supernatural resources any longer. The Bible describes this Fall theologically in these words, "As by one man sin entered into the world, and death by sin, even so death passed upon all men, for all have sinned" (Romans 5:12). Ephesians 4:18 says that man was "alienated from the life of God" in the instant of his Fall. Ephesians 2:1, referring to his spirit, says that man is "dead in trespasses and in sins."

Please note that in the Bible, once a human being has begun to live through conception and birth, he will never experience total death thereafter. The Biblical concept of death is that of separation. In physical death, the individual's soul and spirit are separated from his body. The body dies, but the soul and spirit live on elsewhere. In spiritual death (what Adam experienced the moment he sinned, and what every child of Adam experiences until he is saved), the spirit is separated from God. The spirit dies, but the natural part of the man (everything he received by his first birth) lives on. Tragically, this is the condition of most people on earth today. In eternal death, what the Bible calls "the second death", the individual's separation from God continues in a place called Hell. When an individual dies physically while in a condition of spiritual death, he will experience eternal death in a place of eternal separation from God.

Remember that when Adam sinned, his spirit died instantly and totally, his soul died progressively, and his body died ultimately. It must be noted that when God truly saves a human being from his sins, this Fall is completely reversed.

The spirit of man is saved instantly, totally, and perfectly. The theological terms used for this aspect of salvation are regeneration (the miracle of new birth) and justification (the miracle of God's declaration, on the basis of the death and resurrection of Jesus Christ in the sinner's behalf, that the sinner is both "not guilty" and perfectly righteous and acceptable to God). The soul of man is saved progressively. The theological term for this aspect of salvation is sanctification. And the body is saved ultimately and finally (Romans 8:23). The theological term for this aspect of salvation is glorification.

There are two pillars of absolute perfection in my salvation, the perfect salvation of my spirit (which has already occurred), and the perfect salvation of my body (which will take place instantaneously some time in the future). So one of these perfect pillars of salvation, being past, has already occurred. The other, the "redemption of the body," is yet future, but it will be absolutely perfect when it occurs. Meantime, the daily struggle for sanctification goes on within me at every moment of my life. This sanctification is progressive, and thus it is not perfect, and will never be perfect in this life. So the thoughts, feelings, and choices of my soul are very important in cooperating with God's process of daily sanctification.

At this point, it is necessary to give warning about the possibility of "counterfeit conversion." One of the philosophers said, "Man is incurably religious." Couple that with the fact that man has great capability as a psycho-physical person (soul and body acting together), and you can see that man can do many, many things independently of God. One of these is the practice of religion. His religious instinct drives him to try to make contact with God. The word "religion" comes from a Latin word that means "to bind." Religion is man's attempt to bind himself to God (so it majors on man's works, a man-to-God direction). Here is a shocker: one of the ways man attempts to bind himself to God is in response to the truth of the Gospel of Christ. Remember that man's soul is his mind, emotions, and will, and that he can (and does) exercise that soul without God. So he is capable of making decisions, experiencing feelings, and making choices that are religiously oriented, even Gospel-oriented. We must be careful not to confound that which is truly spiritual and that which is merely soulish or psychical. We have seen that the spirit of man is the sphere of activity where the Holy Spirit operates in the miracle of regeneration. We must also see that the soul is the sphere of activity where Satan operates, making his appeal to the affections and emotions of man. The soul of man (his mind, emotions, and will) is never relationally directed Godward until after man's spirit has been regenerated. Before a man is regenerated, or "born from above" (John 3:3, 7), his soul can only be directed toward himself and the world around him.

Satan knows full well that he dominates the psychical or the soulish man. So he does not care if a man goes to a church where the Spirit of God is not in evidence. He knows that his victim is a creature of emotions, and it matters not if the emotions are stirred to sentimentalism or tears, just so long as man's spirit does not come in contact with God's Holy Spirit. He does not care if man has great religious thoughts, experiences great religious emotions, and makes religious choices -- as long as these things are done independently of the Spirit of God.

Because of this design of Satan, counterfeit conversions can easily occur in any church (and certainly in any religion) at any time, and through any evangelistic effort, just by a human manipulation of the mind, or the emotions, or the will. And the counterfeits usually have such a similarity to the genuine experience that they can easily be substituted for it. Many people have received a "religious inoculation or vaccination." When we are vaccinated, we are given a little of the disease and it keeps us from getting the real thing, the big thing. Thousands of people have just enough religion to "inoculate" them against having a real relationship with Jesus Christ. It is necessary that the counterfeit be identified in order that we may be sure that our conversion experience was genuine.

The first counterfeit conversion is what we might call a *doctrinal* conversion. This is essentially a conversion which occurs only in the mind. A doctrinal conversion is simply a conversion from one set of ideas to another set of ideas. It is a conversion from one set of beliefs to another set of beliefs. For example, here is an atheist. He says that he does not believe in God, in Jesus Christ, in the Bible as the Word of God, in salvation, in immortality, or in any of the doctrines of the Christian faith. But by some means (perhaps by discussion with an intelligent and informed Christian), he one day becomes finally convinced in his mind that these and other doctrines of the Christian faith are true. He makes a public profession of his faith (his new-found belief in the doctrinal truth of the Christian faith), is baptized, and becomes a church member. Was his conversion truly Christian, or was it tragically counterfeit? *Is* he a Christian? *No!* He has merely exchanged one set of ideas for another. He has traded in the idea of atheism for the more satisfying ideas of the New Testament and of the Gospel of Christ. He has new ideas, but he also has the same old sinful heart and the same old untransformed life. He believes intellectually in all the doctrines of the Christian Gospel that are presented to him, but his conversion is only intellectual. This is the kind of "decision" I made (when a pastor explained the Gospel to me). I agreed with all the Gospel propositions mentally (I had no reason to disagree with them), and he told me that I "believed" and thus was "saved." I believed that, too (mentally), and was baptized. However, I was not truly saved until seven years later.

Perhaps a simple illustration will help here. Suppose I go to my doctor and he tells me that I have a vitamin deficiency. He prescribes some vitamins for me to take daily, and I begin to follow his orders. But suppose that one morning I come to the refrigerator to lift the vitamin bottle out. As I do so, the label or wrapper of the bottle comes off in my hand. Holding the wrapper in my hand, I begin to read from it the list of ingredients in the vitamins. It is conceivable that I might become vitamin-starved while reading the contents without taking the tablets themselves. Even so, many take the table of contents of the Christian faith — its doctrines and beliefs — but they do not take Christ Himself as the Redeemer, Savior, and Absolute Lord of their lives. They starve to death spiritually while reading (and mentally believing) the menu! They have been victimized by a "soulish" conversion, a mere conversion of the mind.

No one would dream of confusing a marriage certificate with a marriage. You might hold a marriage certificate without a marriage. You might hold a marriage certificate in your hand all the days of your life and still not be married, and the certificate would be a poor substitute for the relationship.

Many people treat Christianity as primarily a set of interesting moral or religious ideas which can be conveyed by teaching and argument. People cannot be argued into the Kingdom of God, because what is entrusted to the church is not so much a set of ideas as the living reality which lies behind them. It is the crucified, risen and living Christ who stands at the center of the Christian faith — a person, not a mere set of religious propositions.

Mental assent to a set of ideas, rules or beliefs isn't the same as the experience of encountering Jesus Christ. The central question of Christianity is not, "Do you believe this idea or that idea?" but, "who do you say Jesus Christ is?" And once this question is answered adequately and accurately, the big questions are, "What have you done with Him? What is your personal relationship with Him?"

I would not be misunderstood at this point. I am by no means saying that doctrine is unimportant. Doctrine is very, very important, but it is like a signpost which points the way to a real, intimate personal relationship with Jesus Christ. If I wanted to go to Shreveport and did not know the way, a signpost could help me. In fact, the highway sign might be crucial in helping me arrive in Shreveport instead of Monroe. But woe is me if I climb up and sit on the signpost itself, as though that would get me to Shreveport! Doctrines are like signposts that point the way to the Savior. Travelers do not merely give mental assent to the information given by highway signs; they use that information to make the trip! If you have only believed the sign without meeting the Savior, you have had a counterfeit conversion.

Another counterfeit conversion is the merely *emotional* conversion. Of course, this conversion occurs only in the emotions. The emotional conversion is simply a conversion to a feeling, or by a feeling. In this type of counterfeit conversion, feeling is everything. This type of counterfeit conversion is most likely to be experienced by a person who is very high-strung emotionally. The man who has had this type of conversion spends a large part of his life after the conversion trying to feel right. If he feels right, he is confident that all is well between him and God. But if for any reason the feeling is not there, he is miserable, and runs to find it again. He goes to church, to evangelistic services, and to special conferences in order to get the feeling.

Again, an illustration might help to reveal the counterfeit. This is an actual case history, a true story. The person was a small child at the time. She was in an evangelistic meeting one night. In the invitation, the congregation sang a hymn which was deeply moving and packed with emotion. Gripped by the song, the little girl began to cry. The pastor saw her, walked to where she was standing, and asked her if she believed that Jesus Christ died for her sins. Of course she answered, "Yes," because she had been raised in a Christian home and had always believed this. Then the pastor put his hand on her shoulder and led in prayer, thanking God that she had come under conviction of sin. She said years later, "That was where he was wrong. I had experienced no conviction of sin at all. I was crying because the music was sad, the emotional pitch of the service was very high, and the emotion of the moment had gotten me." But the pastor told her that she was converted, and because he said so she had tried to believe it. So another unconverted person was added to the rolls of the church. Fortunately, God later "rescued" her from the "good-faith error" that was made.

Again, I would not be misunderstood. Emotion may be a very vital part of genuine conversion, but it is not equal to conversion, and should not be regarded as the test of conversion. A merely emotional conversion is a counterfeit.

Another counterfeit conversion is the merely *volitional* conversion. This could be called a "moral" conversion. In this type of conversion, a person who has been morally bad wills to become morally good. This is a self-improvement conversion, and multitudes have only this kind. This is the kind of conversion that is often referred to when someone says, "I made a change." This is a conversion to a set of ideals or to a moral standard. It is possible to make a complete moral change and never be converted. In place of one set of conduct patterns, the individual acquires another which is more acceptable and praiseworthy. There is many a man who used to curse, and thought that when he "quit cussin'," that made him a Christian. There is many a man who used to drink, and thought that when he quit drinking, that made him a Christian. This is counterfeit conversion.

The fact of the matter is, a person can be converted to almost anything — to a minister, to a church, to a youth program, to a Sunday School, to some dynamic Christian — but none of these, either singly or together with others, adds up to a Christian conversion.

Since we have spent some time describing counterfeit conversion, let's be sure to also define and describe genuine Christian conversion.

The word "convert" simply means *"to turn."* In fact, the word "conversion" has in it several significant different shades of meaning. (1) It simply means *"to turn around,"* or to do a 180-degree turn. But it also has several accessory ideas in it. (2) It means *"to turn toward"* a certain object or person. The difference is that between a wheel turning on its axis and a flower turning toward the sun. In Christian conversion, the human heart is attracted toward Jesus Christ by the drawing power of the Holy Spirit, just as that flower was attracted to the sun by the warmth of its radiance. (3) It means also *"to turn from one object to another,"* and the two objects are seen to be in direct opposition to each other. So Christian conversion is the turning of the sinner from sin and selfishness to Christ. (4) It means *"to turn back to a point from which it had been turned away."* This introduces another dimension of Christian conversion. So the doctrine of "conversion" has two vital dimensions to it. Christian conversion involves a great one-time crisis that fixes the heart forever on Christ, but it also involves the ongoing process of overcoming all of those seductions of Satan, sin, and the world which would attempt to distract us from Christ. It is like the polar needle of a magnetic compass. It is "fixed" by the manufacturer (just as a Christian was at his conversion!) to always point to polar north (as the Christian was centered on Christ), but there are many other magnetic fields when the compass is in use that may temporarily cause the needle to waver from its "fixed" center, and those distractions must be dealt with if it is to fulfill its purpose. So the doctrine of conversion must include both the crisis at the beginning of the Christian life, and what Sam Shoemaker called "continuing conversion." That magnetic needle may be mechanically forced to point to the south, but as soon as it is freed from the mechanical pressure it will turn automatically again toward the north.

So how shall we define Christian conversion? Christian conversion is what miraculously happens when the inner "center of gravity" in a person shifts (by the work of the Holy Spirit) from himself to Jesus Christ. This is the marvelous and miraculous beginning of God's gracious solution to man's dilemma.

## III. God's Desire for Man

Third, we discover in His Book *God's desire for man*. God's desire for man today begins with a new birth (John 3:3, 7). By means of that miraculous new birth, man becomes a *"partaker of the Divine nature"* (II Peter 1:4). The dynamic Holy Spirit of God re-inhabits the dead human spirit of man and mediates the Presence of Jesus Christ there. When the Holy Spirit produces the new birth, the center of gravity in the person shifts from self to the incoming and indwelling Presence of Christ. When that occurs, that man's inner spirit becomes an extension of the very nature and character of God.

There is a most interesting expression used in Hebrews 12:9. In that verse, God is called "the father of spirits." How intriguing! God is never called the "father" of our souls or our bodies. He is the *creator* of those. But He is called "the *father* of spirits" because He gives birth to the spirit of man in the moment that he receives and trusts Jesus Christ as personal Savior and Lord of his life. How does this occur? John 16:8-11 says that it begins with the conviction of sin. In producing this conviction, the Holy Spirit brings:

1. Strong arguments to your mind,

2. Strong feelings to your emotions, and
3. Strong desires to your will.

The final key is in the will of man and the work God does to change and convince the will. The will stands as a guard at the door of the human spirit. This is the way God sovereignly designed man, and here He determines His work. Jesus said, "Ye will not come to me that ye might have life." But conversely, "Whosoever will may come." The will is the executive of the soul and the guard of the spirit. Jesus said, "As many as received Him, to them gave He power (authority, right) to become the sons of God, even to them that believe on His Name" (John 1:12). The sinner, deeply convicted of his sins, realizes that his only hope is in Christ. The Holy Spirit publicizes Christ to him, and requires him to exercise his awakened will to receive and trust Christ. The will responds with, "I will receive him, I do trust Him," and in that moment, the human spirit is re-inhabited by God. That is the new birth.

So what is God's desire, or God's purpose, for man? The purpose of anything is the reason for which it exists. It is the maker's (the manufacturer's) original intent for making it. The purpose of a thing cannot be discovered by asking another thing. You cannot find out the purpose of a spoon or an automobile by asking another spoon or another automobile. Only the maker (the manufacturer) knows why he created the product the way he did. God is man's Maker, man's Manufacturer, man's Source. Now, every complex product will have a "Manufacturer's Manual" with it, and the manual of operation will explain the purpose, function and operation of the product. Even so, God has provided man with His Manual of Operation, the "Manufacturer's Manual" — the Bible.

The Bible brings man to realistically face the dilemma created by his sin and rebellion against his Maker. It tells us that, due to sin, man's nature and man's thinking are wrong. He is "futile in his thinking, darkened in his understanding, and separated from the life of God because of the ignorance that is in him due to the hardening of his heart" (Ephesians 4:17-18). Man must have a radical readjustment of himself and his thinking. So God commands all men everywhere to repent (Acts 17:30). Repentance means "a change of mind" which brings the person into agreement with God.

Ever since Jesus told the multitudes around Him to repent, many have taken it as an insult that He would imply that their thinking was wrong. Let me be very clear, and I will say it personally about myself. The truth is that no matter how I was thinking before I met Christ, my thinking was wrong. My mind (a part of my soul) had fallen under the administration of Satan and was characterized by ignorance and sin. But "the Lord was patient with me, not willing that I should perish, but that I should come to repentance (a change of mind, heart, character and conduct)" (II Peter 3:9). Out of our Maker's marvelous mercy, He has provided repentance as the means by which we can avoid destruction and return to Him.

The problem with man was that he had become dis-oriented from God through his sin. God had departed from man's inner spirit, and man was "left to his own devices" and his own resources. Because he cannot know in that condition what his purpose is, he will necessarily abuse himself and his total life. The word abuse is a compound word made from the two words, abnormal and use. Any time you are ignorant of the purpose of something, or rebel against its use according to purpose, you end up *abusing* it. This has been the entire history of Godless man.

So, again I ask, What is God's purpose for man? Let me state it in several propositions which arise from the account of man's creation as revealed in "The Manufacturer's Manual."

The Maker tells us that He made man:

1. To contain and communicate the awesome Presence of God;
2. To conquer and control the assigned province God placed him in;
3. To converse and communicate with the amazing Personality of God;
4. To carry and convey an appointed product; and

**5. To continue and consummate an astounding progression.**

Let me explain each of these purposes briefly, reserving the larger discussion to a later time.

1. Man was originally made to contain and communicate the awesome Presence of God. When God made Adam, God dwelt within Adam's human spirit, and God revealed Himself to and through Adam in a completely natural way.
2. Man was originally made to conquer and control the assigned province God placed him in. God said, "Let us make man in our image, in our likeness, and let them have dominion . . ." (Genesis 1:26). "Dominion" is rule, government and control (actually, the Latin word means "lordship"). Man was made to exercise God's control as His deputy.
3. Man was originally made to converse and communicate with the amazing Personality of God. He was created to enjoy fellowship with God.
4. Man was originally made to carry and convey an appointed product. He was created to "be fruitful." He was made to "bear (not produce) fruit" (John 15:1-8). The fruit is essentially character-fruit, "the fruit of

the Spirit" (Galatians 5:22-23). So man was created to contain God and carry ("bear") the fruit God produced from within the man.

5. Finally, man was originally made to continue and consummate an astounding progression. "Be fruitful and multiply." He was to reproduce the life of God-within-him in succeeding generations, thus guaranteeing the extension of that life through all the generations of men. But when he sinned, he instead reproduced his own distorted life (compare Genesis 5:1 and Genesis 5:3 carefully).

Someone wisely said that "life without purpose is merely an experiment." Another said, "Accomplishments without true purpose are a waste of time, energy, and life." This amounts to abuse, or abnormal use, which is all that a person without Christ can do with his life. And unhappily, many people who claim to know Christ are using their lives for no better Christian purpose than if they did not know Him at all.

Several words are used in the Bible to describe God's work in restoring man to his original purpose. One is "regeneration," another is "justification," another is "reconciliation," another is "redemption," another is "adoption," and another is "conversion." Since we have used the word conversion in this study, let me conclude with a summary statement about conversion. Conversion is the establishing in the life of a human being of a right relationship with a living Lord and Savior. Christian conversion means that your life has been brought under the management of Jesus Christ. Robert Munger said it like this: "During the Second World War, thousands of bombing planes were sent on missions of destruction. After the war a few of them were taken over for commercial service. They are called 'converted bombers.' A converted bomber is the same plane that once carried a lethal load of destruction. It has the same wings and fuselage, the same type motors, the same cockpit and instrument panel. But there are several differences. The bomb racks are gone. The gun turret is gone. The plane now has a new owner. It carries new cargo. It has a new pilot. This is true conversion."

Even so, if you have been truly converted to Christ, you have a new owner and a new pilot, and you carry a new cargo. Almighty God now owns your life; its pilot is Jesus Christ, who guides and controls you through the indwelling of the Holy Spirit; and you now have a new direction, new ambitions, new dynamic, and new resources for the living of an abundant life in Christ. This is why Dr. E. Y. Mullins called conversion "the Christian life in germ form." In it is concentrated all of the elements of the Christian life which follows. So conversion installs into the believer that DNA, all the spiritual genes and chromosomes of the Christian life which follows.

Charles Simeon, the great Cambridge pastor, was asked about the process of conversion. He wrote, "Conversion is completely contrary to the course of nature, and can only be brought about by God's almighty power. Before conversion, the person's heart and mind flow steadily downward — away from his Creator, by a natural tendency — toward destruction. After conversion, all its tendencies are changed, and it flows upwards from destruction, back again toward its Creator. Is this due to mere human agency? Certainly not! All the resources, all the capabilities, all the efforts of all the inhabitants of the globe could not do it. It is done by the invisible, infinite, miraculous power of God."

When a person is converted to Christ, regenerated by the Spirit of God, born from above, his human spirit, which was dead because of sin, is re-inhabited by the Holy Spirit of God and "quickened" into Divine Life. Then, God is "in business" in that person again!

*Chapter 5*

# THE MISERY OF MAN

## *Genesis 3:1-24*

Why is the world, as we now know it, a mixture of beauty and brokenness? Why are human beings, as they now are, a mixture of dignity and degradation? Why is God, as He is presently disposed toward us as a race, so near and yet so distant, to be passionately loved and yet also to be legitimately feared, merciful and wrathful, loving and judging? In the third chapter of Genesis we have the Biblical explanation of all of this, with its account of the fall of the human race in Adam from its place of high honor and safety to its present disgrace and insecurity.

The third chapter of Genesis in the Bible gives us the world's greatest commentary on several key concepts of human experience. First, it is a great commentary about the existence and character and purpose of *Satan*, the archenemy of God, man, truth and holiness. Then, it is a great commentary on *sin*, its seduction and its sequel.

Then, Genesis three provides great insight into the Biblical understanding of *salvation* from sin and its effects. There is hardly a great doctrine of Christianity that does not have some introduction and some interpretation in Genesis three. One great commentator called it "the greatest single chapter in the Bible for understanding so many ultimate things." In this study, we will focus our attention mainly on the person, purposes and activities of "his infernal majesty, the devil." The other themes will trail Satan into our study.

One of the first rules of warfare is to "know your enemy". If we want to dissect Satan's strategy, the best way to do it is to return to the place where it was first on display. That place is the Garden of Eden, and the story is best told in Genesis chapter three. So we will focus our attention today on The Misery of Man as it is documented in that great chapter of the Bible.

## I. The Circumstances of the Misery of Man

First, the third chapter of Genesis reveals *the circumstances* of the fall of man. The first of the circumstances of man's fall into sin and Satan's control is the *perfect place* where that fall occurred. What an idyllic scene! The first account of man's life is a love story, the first romance of the human race. There is a perfect start of a perfect couple in a perfect environment. And the scene ends in a tragedy! The first temptation and sin of man occurred in a perfect paradise. Those who contend that if man were given the right environment, the right "climate" for living, he would emerge as a paragon of virtue and morality are wrong. The first sin occurred in paradise.

Consider these advantages in the story of the first human beings: Adam and Eve were physically perfect. Adam and Eve had full and perfect knowledge of God's revealed will. Adam and Eve were perfectly mated. Adam and Eve dwelt in a perfect paradise with every need satisfied. In fact, the Garden seems to have been provided to accommodate them. And yet they tragically fell when opportunity came.

Think of the personal participants in the story. Genesis 2:15-17 says that "The LORD God took the man, and put him into the garden of Eden to dress it and to keep it. And the LORD God commanded the man, saying, Of every tree of the garden you may freely eat: But of the tree of the knowledge of good and evil, you shall not eat of it: for in the day that you eat thereof, you shall surely die." Then the Biblical text tells us of the formation of Eve (Genesis 2:19-23). These are the two main human participants in the story of the fall. Up to a certain entry-point, Adam is not seen in Genesis three (Adam is first referred to in the last part of verse 6). Genesis 3:1 says, "And he (Satan using the serpent as his agent of communication) said unto the woman, ...." According to the text, the person first tempted was Eve. We will discuss the importance of this fact later in this study.

As the exchange between Satan and Eve progresses, Eve corrects Satan's statements twice, but with two features which betray a gradually wavering trust in God. For example, when Satan said, "Has God said, You shall not eat of every (in effect, any) tree of the garden?" Eve replied, "We may eat of the fruit of the trees of the garden," but she omitted God's use of the word "every" in his original communication (remember that

God gave one exception to that rule, the "tree of the knowledge of good and evil"—Genesis 2:17). So Eve's first waver was by means of omission of a significant word from God. Then, in verse 3, Eve said, "But of the fruit of the tree which is in the midst of the garden, God has said, You shall not eat of it, neither shall you touch it, lest ye die." Here, Eve further wavers before Satan's subtle suggestions—twice. Once, she wavered by addition. She added a stipulation to the clearly stated requirement of God. God had said nothing about "touching" the fruit of the tree. Then, Eve also wavered by alteration of the word of God. God had said, "In the day you eat thereof, you shall surely die." Eve reduced this clear declaration of a certain revealed dire penalty to a mere threat of this penalty. Do you see, dear friend, that Satan pursues this subtle strategy to this day (more about this later). He seeks to secure omissions of some of the words of God in our thinking, as well as additions to the words of God based on our own preferred thinking, and finally, complete alterations of the words of God. In the first temptation of human beings, Eve is the tempted party.

I mention just one feature of Satan's appeal in the story as we focus momentarily on the other key participant in the temptation of Eve. Apparently the Original Recorder, the Holy Spirit, intended us to notice and understand this feature. Though the usual name for God in Genesis two and three is Jehovah Elohim, or "the LORD God" (used 19 times in these two chapters), Satan does not and apparently cannot use that name. Instead, Satan merely refers to Him by the second of these two names, Elohim, translated merely by the word "God". This is urgently important in understanding Satan and the nature of his temptation. In verse three, Eve echoes Satan, showing growing agreement of thought and direction with him, and calls God merely by the name "Elohim". Elohim is the

Hebrew name for God as mighty, powerful, all-controlling, all-creating, but apparently distant. The name "Jehovah" is the name for God as the loving and gracious covenant Partner of His people. Satan could not make this concession; it would have been too great a reminder to Eve of God's real purposes. When Eve conceded to Satan's words by using only the name "Elohim" to refer to God, she further crumbled before his sly schemes. The serpent subtly crossed her path—and left the serpent's slime in his trail—and Eve slipped on it, right into Satan's trap. The second personal participant in this story of man's fall is Satan himself. We will discuss Adam only after he appears in the story (at verse 6).

The third circumstance of the fall I would mention is the plain prohibition declared by God as He stated His "rules for the Garden." In Genesis 2:16-17, God said, "Of every tree of the garden you may freely eat: But of the tree of the knowledge of good and evil, you shall not eat of it: for in the day that you eat thereof, you shall surely die." Note that God began with a generous permission, and only followed that gracious statement with the single prohibition. He set them wonderfully free to enjoy the garden, with only one tiny test to secure the moral bounds of their relationship with Him. Someone sadly said, "With every delight in the garden as their permitted privilege, they lost it all by choosing one bite of the forbidden fruit!"

Note also that the construction of Eve (Genesis 2:18-23) came *after* God gave this prohibition to *Adam*. Adam is the assigned representative of the human race, the responsible man, and the one in whom the race stands or falls (on the basis of a simple and seemingly easy test), so God expresses the allowance and the prohibition to Adam only.

The final circumstance of the fall that I would mention at this point is the *possible purpose* in God's sovereignty and permission regarding the fall of man into sin. Why did God cause this situation, and thus allow man's fall? "God tempts not any man, nor can He Himself be tempted by evil" (see James 1:13). Let me say it again lest you don't see it: God is not the author of sin. Satan, Adam and Eve are each created beings, made by God Himself, but they were not created as sinful or evil beings. By what allowance, then, and for what purpose did God allow the Garden of Eden episode?

God orchestrated the test of Eve and then Adam in the Garden of Eden to test man's respect for God's right to be God. I'm sure that some readers of this study have deliberately and determinedly and intentionally looked for loopholes at every line of the study. Dear friend, does not your innate, self-favoring, sinful bias prove the point: you simply do not want to concede to God the right to be God. Though He does not wait on your vote to be Himself or exercise His sovereign rights over the universe, indeed, over you, you still vainly hold out for your usurpation of His position. You still want to "be as God" (Genesis 3:5) without God. Of course, you don't see this as High Treason committed flagrantly and rebelliously against the throne of the universe—but God does!

The basic test of Eden was *a test of wills*. Whose will is to be ascendant, dominant and determinant? This is the acid test, this is the "litmus" test, of all of moral life, and this is the final indicator of man's alignment in life. If Adam had passed this test (more about this later, also), he would have passed "from glory to glory" in the everlasting life of relationship with God. But, alas…. again, a word to the skeptic: if you do not admit such truths, how solid, how satisfying, how reasonable, how substantial, is *your explanation* of the disastrous (!!!) history of man? If you retain your skepticism against all apparent reality, I would suggest that you read (or re-read) both the story, <u>Lord of the Flies</u>, and the philosophical history of the author, William Golding. What an education in the inevitable facing of the objective moral realities that prevail in the world in which we live! And this is only to mention *one* of many such excursions into reality and revelations of that reality in the realm of world literature.

You see, dear friend, man was not created *righteous*, but merely *innocent*. *Innocence*, though wonderful, is basically *negative* (marked by the absence of many, many things, including the grandeur of tested and proven morality), while true *righteousness* (a massive, massive word in the Bible, and first used to define and describe *God*) is always *positive* (fully tested, fully proven, and finally, fully perfect). So, though Adam and Eve were in paradise, it was necessary that they be placed on probation there.

These, then, are some of the circumstances of the fall of the human race into sin. Now, we will progress further.

## II. The Components of the Misery of Man

Now, we will examine more of the *components* of the fall of man into sin as they are presented in Genesis three.

The first component I would mention here is *the tempter*, the one who induced man to sin. Let me cite several verses which "unwrap" Satan for our examination of his character and conduct.

Revelation 12:9 echoes the Genesis three story with these words: "And the great dragon was cast out, that old serpent, called the Devil, and Satan, who deceives the whole world, and his angels were cast out with him." What a condensed package of truth about Satan! In John 8:44, Jesus, referring to our Genesis three story, said to the Pharisees (the most moral and religious people of His day), "You are of your father the devil, and the lusts (drives, works) of your father you will do. He was a murderer from the beginning, and abode not in the truth, because there is no truth in him. When he speaks a lie, he speaks of his own: for he is a liar, and the father of it." II Corinthians 4:3-4 says, "If our Gospel is veiled, it is veiled to those who are lost, in whom the god of this world has blinded the minds of them which believe not, lest the light of the glorious Gospel of Christ, who is the image of God, should shine unto them." In I Peter 5:8-9, Scripture counsels us to "be serious, be watchful, for your adversary the devil, as a roaring lion, goes about, seeking whom he may devour." II Corinthians 11:3 says, "I fear, lest by any means, as the serpent beguiled Eve through his subtlety, so your minds should be corrupted from the simplicity that is in Christ." In I Timothy 2:13-14, Paul wrote to his disciple Timothy, "And Adam was not deceived, but the woman was deceived." II Corinthians 11:14 says, "Satan himself is transformed into an angel of light." II Corinthians 2:11 says, "Lest Satan should get an advantage of us; for we are not ignorant of his devices." Incidentally, the word "devices" here suggests mental processes, perceptions and purposes. In Ephesians 6:11, Paul wrote, "Put on the whole armor of God, that you may be able to stand against the wiles of the devil." Here, the word "wiles" means "schemes" or "tricks". In this verse and the next (verse 12), the word "against" is used six times, emphasizing the very real conflict between good and evil, between Satan and God (with man as the main battlefield). God and Satan are irreconcilably opposed to each other, and God will not lose this battle. These verses "undress" and "expose" Satan, and allow us see into his heart.

Let me note the fact that Satan is not mentioned in the first two chapters of the Bible. In the first verse of the third chapter from the beginning, he is introduced as "the serpent" (Genesis 3:1). Then he is not mentioned in the last two chapters of the Bible. In the third from the last chapter in the Bible, he is mentioned for the final time, as "that old serpent the devil" (Revelation 20:2). This silence regarding Satan is crucial, but the evidence of his person, his work, and his effects may be clearly seen on almost every page between the two chapters at the beginning and the two chapters at the end which are marked by his absence.

Let me also note that Satan speaks a grand total of only three times in the Bible, and in each case, the text of the report could occupy the lifetime study of a diligent student. His speech is recorded in Genesis chapter three, in Job chapters one and two, and in Matthew chapter four (and the other accounts of the Temptation of Jesus in the Gospels). There is an almost ascending revelation in these three occurrences of Satan's speech. In Genesis three, Satan slanders God to man. In Job, Satan slanders man to God. And in the Gospel accounts of the Temptation of Jesus, at God's initiative, Satan is brought face to face with the God-Man, Jesus. We must realize this rule: *Satan tempts* man to bring him to *destruction; God tests* man to produce and reveal *holiness of character.* Here, then, is a quick look at the tempter in the temptation account.

Now, I will quickly mention the tool of the tempter, the serpent. Verse one says, "Now the serpent was more subtle than any beast of the field which the Lord God had made." The word "subtle" means "crafty." Please note that the serpent was not lowly and loathsome when Satan used it as his agent to tempt Eve. The serpent was not then as most of us think of it now. The present snake reveals the marks of the curse of God after Adam and Eve sinned (read Genesis 3:14 carefully, where God confronted the serpent and cursed it). That cursed character of the serpent is a caricature of the original, just as the present perverted nature of man is a terribly distorted caricature of his original nature. Satan would never employ as his tool on a mission of appeal a creature that was ugly and forbidding. No, the serpent was quite apparently a splendid, beautiful, attractive, disarming creature. Indeed, it probably was an upright creature at this time, as suggested by the nature of the curse God pronounced upon it—"upon your belly you shall go."

Remember that Satan's original name was "Lucifer," which means "light-bearer," or the "bright and shining one." We are told that he was originally full of wisdom and perfect in beauty, and that he was apparently great in authority and position at the beginning (see Ezekiel 28:12-17). Here, Satan, the fallen angel, seeks to reassume his original attractiveness in order to be very appealing to Eve. In doing so, he adopted a splendid and subtle creature as his agent. The serpent became the tool of the tempter.

At this point, I will address the *temptation* itself. Look at the mechanics of Satan's timely approach. First, Satan began with the woman, the weaker vessel (see I Peter 3:7). Second, Satan approached Eve when she was alone, without Adam's support. Only later is Adam addressed as present. Third, Satan approached Eve when she was in full sight of the tree. "When she saw the tree…" Fourth, Satan was careful to not appear in a form that would terrorize or traumatize her or arouse her suspicion. Instead, as mentioned, he chose as his instrument an extremely attractive animal. Fifth, Satan advanced by degrees, to obtain a footing in her heart. An old Arab proverb says, "If the camel ever gets his nose in the tent, the entire camel will soon be inside." Sixth, Satan did not shock Eve by suggesting some blatant blasphemy of God, only the harmless, pleasant gratification of natural desire—but out of the will of God. Furthermore, he used only obscure and ambiguous language. What he said meant one thing to him, but quite a different, more appealing, thing to Eve. And finally, Satan gave no impression of being the fixed enemy of God. True, his references to God were derogatory, but only subtly, not blatantly. In fact, he pretended to be seeking her good. So the word "subtle" or "crafty" assumes full meaning here.

Now, think of the *tricky appeal* Satan made. First, he *insinuated a subtle doubt* into Eve's mind. "He said unto the woman, 'Yea, has God said, You shall not eat of every tree of the garden?" "Surely, now," said Satan, "God would not be such a tyrant as to take away your pleasures. How loving could any God be who would make such a prohibition as that?" Thus, he subtly discounted the goodness of God. Doesn't seem like much of a step, does it? Ah, but it is the beginning of doubt for Eve, and it creates momentum in the direction of unbelief.

The second facet of his appeal was to *insert a significant distortion* into her mind. "Has God said ....You shall not eat of every tree of the garden?" Actually, God had said nothing of the sort, but Satan slyly magnified and enlarged God's restrictions. He minimized God's permission ("of every tree of the garden you may freely eat") and magnified God's prohibition, making it look far worse by declaring that God had made all the trees of the garden off limits to the human pair. Remember that Jesus was referring to this account when he said of Satan, "He is a liar," and labeled him "the father of lies" (John 8:44).

Third, Satan injected a straightforward denial into Eve's thinking. Genesis 3:4 says, "The serpent said unto the woman, 'You shall not surely die.'" As it turned out, this seemed at worst to be a half-truth, for they did not die physically for a long time. But they did die! They died in trespasses and sins. They died spiritually. They died in relationship to God. Though their bodies remained alive (and possibly healthy) and their souls remained alive (and possibly happy), they died instantly and perfectly in their spirits (the instrument of relationship with God in a man). The Holy Spirit of God evacuated the human spirit of man, and his spirit became an instant death chamber. But Satan boldly denied the word of God, saying, "You shall not surely die." Is he not doing this around the clock every day somewhere on planet earth, convincing men that they need not fear at all the deadly consequences of sin? "After all, there is no hell. If there is a God and there is a hell, He is too good to permit anyone to go there." The main issue of human existence, the crucial issue of sin, is thus resolved by an easy-going glibness that removes moral judgment from God's universe. "Be not deceived; God is not mocked. For whatever a man sows, that shall he also reap" (Galatians 6:7). Since I have probably raised the hackles of the cynic by mentioning the taboo word, "hell", let me state the rationale of Scripture concerning the place. The great crime of humanity is that we choose to live without reference to our Maker. The punishment is that God grants us what we wish. Hell is the greatest compliment God ever paid to man's very serious free will.

The final movement of Satan's appeal to Eve was to impose a strong deceit into the entire episode. Satan said, "Ye shall not surely die: For God knows that in the day you eat thereof, then your eyes shall be opened, and you shall be as God, knowing good and evil." Satan, the father of lies, professes to know the mind of the God of truth, and presumes to speak for Him! He made two promises: (1) "Your eyes shall be opened" and you shall "know good from evil" (verse 5). And indeed, both promises were fulfilled, though not as they thought. Satan's first promise was fulfilled, for verse seven says, "And the eyes of them both were opened. . . .knowing good and evil," but not as they thought. (2) "You shall be like God," said Satan, using the word he and Eve shared in labeling God (the word "Elohim," the Creator God, but not coupled with Jehovah, the Covenant God of His people). This is the ultimate Adamic fallacy, the ultimate deceit, the ultimate blasphemy, that man by himself can achieve God-likeness. But note that it certainly appeared that man had achieved that goal. Verse 22 says, "And the LORD God said, 'Behold, the man has become as one of us, to know good and evil." Before we examine the meaning of God's words here, let us see that, as in Genesis 1:26 when the Trinity jointly planned the creation of man, here again the Members of the Trinity hold intimate council to determine the expulsion of Adam and Eve from the Garden (note the word "us" here).

What do God's statements mean? Satan's promises were fulfilled, as he planned, only with modifications. "Your eyes shall be opened, to know good from evil." Note the enticing thought that the fruit of the tree in the center of the Garden of Eden was Knowledge. To Eve, the temptation did not come from the fruit, but from the prospect of a larger life. So Satan tempted Eve to rise to a higher life ("you shall be like God") and to expand into a larger life—not to fall to a lower, more restricted life. His offer was for her to rise upward, not fall downward! Bible commentator Henry Morris wrote, "Man had once known only the goodness of God; but now he had come to know experimentally the evil inherent in rejecting

God's Word, as well as the necessary spiritual and physical suffering resulting from such action, so that he did, indeed, 'know good and evil.'" They knew good, but without the power to do it, and they knew evil, but without the power to shun it. So, whether they knew it or not, they could never again in their fallen state fully love good and shun evil. They were morally crippled and could not overcome that infirmity.

So they became "like God"—but certainly not as they anticipated. Verse 22 continues, "And the LORD God said, Behold, the man is become as one of us, to know good and evil: and now, lest he put forth his hand, and take also of the tree of life, and eat, and live forever...." Though "Godness" was promised by Satan, the product was only a pitiful caricature of what Adam and Eve had anticipated. They now could develop a "sophisticated knowledge" which is independent of God, a knowledge that would become brilliance but without corresponding wisdom. In the contemporary western culture of today, the "civilized" descendants of Adam and Eve are everywhere evident; one has only to compare the "advances" of our culture with that of the "brilliant" Germans in a highly educated and advanced culture—who succumbed to Adolph Hitler! Biblically, this knowledge of good and evil becomes the "wisdom that is from beneath" pitted against God's knowledge, the "wisdom that is from above" (to pursue this theme further, read James 3:15-17 and I Corinthians 1:18-31).

You see, God knows the full range of sin's consequences better than any sinner does (sin both binds the person in selfishness and blinds him to reality, God's "true Truth"—always), and if He did not practice prevenient grace toward sinners, a grace that prevents the worst penalties of sin immediately occurring, who could be saved? "So he (the LORD

God) drove out the man; and He placed at the east of the garden of Eden, Cherubims, and a flaming sword which turned every way, to keep (guard) the way of the tree of life" (verse 24). Henry Morris again wrote, "It would have been calamitous had they continued in a perfect environment as sinful people, especially eating the fruit of the tree of life and living on indefinitely in such a condition." So, in order to prevent man from living forever in increasing sin and its attending penalty (which will occur in Hell—man will live in "the Eternal Now" in increasing sin and its attending penalty), God precluded their contact with the tree of life. So His "punitive" action in dismissing them from the Garden was first of all an act of remarkable mercy. Mercy means that the sinner does not get what he deserves—and this was certainly true after the sin of Adam and Eve.

Now, we will look at the transgression itself. One sin led to the expulsion of Adam and Eve from paradise; how can you, with your many, many sins hope to get into God's Paradise—unless you hasten to appropriate His provision for salvation? What was the nature of Adam's one deadly sin? God simplified the test: to eat of the forbidden fruit, or not to eat of it. That was the issue. But what was the real transgression? What was the meaning of the act of eating the prohibited fruit? It meant an instantaneous shift of the center of gravity within Adam. In that instant, he moved from Theonomy (the rule of God as the inward law of his life) to Autonomy (the establishment of self-law as the ruling principle of his life). This arrogance, this pride, this self-curl, is the nature and essence of all sin. Sin, you see, is the set (fixation, focus) on self that was the immediate and ensuing result of their act of disobedience. "Every man has turned to his own way," the Bible says (Isaiah 53:6). Sin is the determination that I will live by my own preferred rules. It is the decision to make my will central and God's will peripheral (if I even allow His will to occupy a place in my thoughts at all). So a life in sin is not necessarily a scandalous life; it might be a very respected, humanly useful and humanly admired life. But if it is God-less it is profoundly sinful. Sin is a flight from, a rebellion against, and an antipathy to God, where self is central and supreme. Sin is not simply a broken code but a broken relationship; not only a relationship lost but a relationship renounced.

So, in the tense exchange between Satan and Eve, with Adam brought into the act by Eve's offer of the forbidden fruit to him, a pattern was followed. The guilty pair moved from *Theocentrism (being God-centered) to eccentrism (being off-centered) to autocentrism (being self-centered).* Adam and Eve took the bait to become their own gods, thus displacing God with puny, pusillanimous, pygmy, but *pitifully proud, SELF.* Putting himself in a position of moral defiance toward his Creator, man plunged himself into a life of tension and absolute moral uncertainty (unless God intervenes), unable to control himself or his world. Self-consciousness tragically replaced God-consciousness. One of the immediate consequences of the fall was that Adam and Eve began to evade responsibility for their own misdeeds (see Genesis 3:11-13); man's endless blame-game began in Eden.

Sin began in Eve's *agreement with Satan.* Adam and Eve sinned when they listened to and obeyed the voice of Satan. Salvation, on the other hand, begins in man's agreement with God. A sinner is saved when he listens to and obeys the voice of God. But this is only possible when a sinful human being is miraculously brought into agreement with God. Romans 10:9 says, "If you shall confess (Greek, homologeses, to "say the same thing; agree with") with your mouth that Jesus is Lord, and believe in your heart that God has raised Him from the dead, you shall be saved." Read that sentence several times and with great care before proceeding on in this study. Salvation is yours when you are brought by the Holy Spirit into full agreement with God about Jesus and His saving work for you. Dear Christian, if you know anything about the deep-seated depravity of your own heart, then you know that a full-scale miracle was necessary for you to be saved! Indeed, the terms used for your salvation in the Bible—a re-creation, a birth, a resurrection—reveal the full nature of this full miracle.

Before we proceed to the next major point, let me construct a supposition. Suppose Adam had resisted the temptation that came to him through Eve's offer of the forbidden fruit which she had just eaten. What would have happened? I think we can safely and fairly draw this conclusion: Eve would have been lost, but the human race would not have been lost. As sentimental as we may naturally be about our first parents, hoping that they were truly saved (and there is divided opinion at this point), God could have made another woman (or another man, had the person in question been Adam). But the race did not stand in EVE; it stood in ADAM. The full tragedy of the Garden of Eden followed the sin of Adam, not the sin of Eve, because Adam was the assigned representative of the human race. Romans 5:12 says, "As by one man sin entered into the world, and death by sin, so death passed upon all men, for all sinned." If Adam had resisted the temptation to sin, man would have gone on in righteousness, not merely in innocence, and would have forever enjoyed an ascending romance ("from glory to glory") with the Infinite God of Glory.

## III. The Cure for the Misery of Man

We will conclude our study of Genesis three by looking for the *cure* for the fall of man as that cure is seen in this chapter. Before God dealt with Adam and Eve in judgment, He first made a promise of mercy and then enacted a clear picture of His coming redemption.

First, His cure for man's fall was *clearly stated in the first Gospel prophecy.* The moment of man's transgression was barely past when God spoke in mercy. His statement was decisively and powerfully addressed to Satan, but Adam and Eve eaves-dropped on His words to Satan. God's astounding declaration presented in a nutshell the entire Divine plan of human redemption. Amazingly, it was given at the very dawn of human history, shortly after man had sinned. In Genesis 3:15, God said to Satan, "And I will put enmity between you and the woman, and between your seed and her seed; it shall bruise your head, and you shall bruise his heel." This prophecy has been called the "Protevangelium", or "the first Gospel." Another called it "the Gospel in embryo." The statement is even more replete than it appears in a first reading. At least six participants in the coming drama of redemption are identified in the verse. While remaining within my purpose in this study, I want to mention only four of them: *Satan*, the woman (*Eve*), with a slight suggestion of another woman, the mother of the single Seed to come (*Mary*, the mother of Jesus), and the woman's single seed-to-come (*Christ Himself*).

These specific realities command our attention in this incredible verse: a spiritual conflict is initiated here ("I, God, will put hostility between you and the woman, and between your seed and her seed"); two specific combatants are identified here ("he," referring to the coming champion, and "you," referring to Satan); a special champion is introduced here ("her seed", gender-identified as "he"); a singular contest is indicated here ("He will bruise your head, and you shall bruise his heel"); and a significant conquest is implied here ("He will crush your head"). Note the masculine pronoun in the last sentence, and notice the full and final coming victory of "the Seed of the woman" (the virgin-born Savior, Jesus Christ) over Satan.

Again we can see a succession of extremely strange things either implied or stated in this verse: a strange birth (a coming single Seed will appear in history, miraculously born as "the seed of the woman"), a strange Baby (the "Seed" which came through that birth), a strange battle ("...enmity between..."), two strange bruisings ("He shall bruise your head, you shall bruise his heel"; crucifixion is the only means of capital punishment ever known to man in which the victim's heel is ALWAYS bruised!!! ), and a strange blessing (eternal salvation for sinners emerges in time and history from this "succession of extremely strange things!").

These Gospel realities may be detected in this one verse: (1) We find here God's initiation of the conviction in the hearts of sinners that leads to their salvation. God said, "I will put enmity (hostility) ...." Blaise Pascal, the brilliant French mathematician, scientist, philosopher and theologian, rightly said, "The most cruel war which God can make with men in this life is to leave them without that war which He came to bring." If God does not initiate this hostility by prevenient grace into sinners' hearts, not one sinner would ever be saved. (2) We see here both the first and second comings of Christ. In His first coming, His heel was bruised (He suffered a serious blow in His Death on the Cross, but the wound was not irreversible; He arose from the dead). This is history. In His second coming, He will finally and forever crush the serpent's (Satan's) head. A crushed head is an irreversible, fatal wound! This is yet unfulfilled prophecy, though the "death-blow" was administered by Christ to Satan on the Cross. (3) We see also the virgin birth of Christ. Note the peculiar expression "the seed of the woman," referring to an individual, a coming male ("he") champion. Everyone knows that the human race is propagated through the seed of the man, never through the seed of a woman. The latter expression invents an idea totally unknown except in one Person, the virgin-born Savior, Jesus Christ. No other person in human history was ever born merely of a virgin woman without the biological, sexual agency of a man. (4) We also see the atoning Death of Christ on the Cross. Again, this is the meaning of the bruising of His heel in this verse. (5) We can note the resurrection of Christ in this verse. His heel is bruised (His Death), but He later finally and fully crushes the serpent's head (presupposing His resurrection after He died). (6) The declaration of Satan's defeat and doom—"He (Christ) will crush your (Satan's) head." The crushing of the head refers to a fatal, irreversible wound. (7) The necessity of regeneration to be saved. Man is born as "the seed of the serpent" in his first birth into the fallen human family (see Psalm 51:5 & John 8:44), but at his regeneration, or second birth (a birth as real, as radical, as revolutionary as his first birth, a birth in which a previously non-existent person comes into being), he is "born again," or "born from above" and by means of this new birth he is instantly and permanently placed in God's Forever Family. (8) Salvation by a God-sent Champion who saves by substituting Himself in the place of sinners and paying for them the sin-debt that they could not pay. He was "bruised for our iniquities"

(Isaiah 53:5). All of this in a single verse, and that verse contains God's first response to man's fall!

Finally, God's cure for man's fall may be clearly seen in a Gospel picture. Genesis 3:6 says, "Eve took of the fruit and ate, and gave also unto her husband with her, and he ate, also. And the eyes of them both were opened, and they knew that they were naked; and they sewed fig leaves together, and made themselves aprons." Later, the text says, "Unto Adam also and to his wife did the LORD God make coats of skins, and clothed them" (verse 21). This account is a classic Old Testament "type" (the Greek word used in the New Testament is tupos, which means an "exact impress," or a "pattern") of a New Testament reality. Here, in a simple and strange picture, we find the entire plan of human redemption in miniature. We will briefly explore the dimensions of the type.

When Adam and Eve experienced the distress of guilt, they instinctively sought covering. Though naked before, they knew no shame or guilt. But since their fall, they were driven to hide themselves and their nakedness. First, they attempted to cover their new-felt guilt and shame by sewing fig leaves together to make aprons (verse 6). One commentator says that their attempt to cover themselves was only "the external reflex of the internal nakedness of the sin-burdened mind before God." Then, "Adam and his wife hid themselves from the presence of the LORD God among the trees of the garden" (verse 8). But they found that the fig-leaves and the trees were too slight a covering for so deep a shame.

Pastor Ray Pritchard pictured the sinner's handicap in these graphic words: "Imagine taking your best dress or your best suit and dragging it through the mud. Then you put it on the floor where people can walk on it. Then you use it to mop up your dog's vomit. Then you put on the suit and drive to the most expensive restaurant in your town. With such sights and smells on your person, what will they say when you come to the door? You will immediately be turned away. 'But I have a reservation,' you cry out. It matters not. You are not dressed appropriately to enter this exclusive restaurant. 'Get out,' the doorman says, 'or I'll call the police.' How do you think God feels when you stand before him dressed in the dirty rags of your own 'good' deeds? What looks good to you is worse than a vomit-streaked garment in His pure eyes." In fact, dear friend, your "good deeds" may be regarded as "good" by many, many people on this renegade outpost called Earth, but they are non-negotiable as currency for entrance into the King's Realm.

Author Roger Carswell added this perceptive insight to the account: "Just as the cloak of Christ was gambled for at the cross, and then presumably worn by somebody to whom it did not belong, so too, a falsely-assumed righteousness (or even the name of Christ) has often been taken by those who have no true righteousness such as God requires, or they falsely profess His righteousness though they are strangers to it in relationship and experience. The way they 'wear' it only abuses it. If, going directly against your instructions, I murdered in your name, are you to blame? Surely not! A Christian will feel deeply that all men, being sinners, need to come to Christ in repentance and faith, but he is not going to fight someone who doesn't! Rather he will want to love that person all the more."

Following the same illustrative theme, evangelist Gordon Bayless wrote, "We do not know the name of the Roman soldier who won the robe of Christ at the cross, but we do know this: if he had known what you and I know today, he might have asked Christ and the Savior would have given him the robe of His own righteousness to wear all the way home to Heaven. The entire earthly wardrobe of Christ was never worth more than a few of our American dollars—robes that would turn to dust in a few years. Today, men gamble in the presence of Jesus for things that have no more value than the clothing Jesus wore on the day before His crucifixion. 'If you knew the gift of God, and Who it is Who says to you, Here is My Righteousness, take it by faith, free of charge, and My Father will accept you as if you were Me, you would ask for it and receive it in an instant!'"

In a sermon on the New Testament doctrine of justification, Charles Spurgeon said, "The covering for man's sin cannot be of man's doing. Man is like a silkworm. He is a spinner and weaver by night, operating in the dimness of a world darkened by sin. A robe of righteousness is wrought out for him, but he will not have it. He will spin for himself, and like the silkworm, he spins and spins, and he only spins himself a shroud. All the righteousness a sinner can make will only be a shroud in which to wrap up his soul, his destroyed soul, for God will cast away that man who refuses His provision and relies upon his own works."

Genesis 3:21 says, "Unto Adam also and to his wife did the LORD God make coats of skins, and clothed them." Don't hurry past this statement in the text of this crucial chapter; it contains a remarkable picture of a sinner's hope of Heaven. Adam and Eve had instinctively tried to cover their own shame and guilt by sewing fig leaves together (verse 7) to cover their nakedness. But the covering they provided, though an acknowledgment of real need, was not adequate for so great a need as the guilt caused by human sin. God disregarded their attempt as completely inadequate, but without accusation or charge, He made His own provision of a covering that *was* sufficient. What was the difference between "fig leaves" and the "coats of skins?" Why were the fig leaves fruitless and the skins-for-sins adequate? What a strange puzzle!

Isaiah 64:6 records this shattering truth: "We are all as an unclean thing, and all our righteousnesses (note the plural form of the word 'righteousness,', speaking of the total of the very best any human being can offer) are as filthy rags; and we all do fade as a leaf; and our iniquities, like the wind, have taken us away." God's perfect righteousness and man's perverted "righteousness" are two utterly different kinds of righteousness. We tend to think of God's righteousness as merely better or purer than ours, and that intent and effort may improve ours to match His. Let me say firmly that this is by no means the case! The righteousness of God and the supposed "righteousness" of man are totally different in kind, not merely in degree. Human righteousness is not just a lesser form of Divine righteousness, inferior but adjustable to meet God's standard. No, no, no! No righteousness of man that is independent of God's grace and God's salvation will ever gain acceptance in Heaven.

It is a standing procedure with Heaven's God to reject any attempt by sinful human beings to make themselves presentable or acceptable to Him, because "God is of purer eyes than to behold iniquity" (Habakkuk 1:13). However, this Divine determination is overmatched by God's own willingness to provide for sinners by His own free grace the only means of acceptance with Himself which He can honor. God demands perfect righteousness for admission to His Presence, but man does not have in himself such righteousness. Therefore, God graciously supplies to man what He demands of him. Here are the dimensions of His provision as pictured in Genesis 3:21.

First, the LORD God did it; He provided the sufficient covering for the flagrant transgressions of Adam and Eve.

Second, Death was necessary to supply the means of covering. An innocent animal had to die and be skinned. How did the animal die? Not naturally, but violently, by blood-letting, apparently as a God-ordained sacrifice (see Hebrews 4:1-7). The animal did not die to provide food for sustenance, but to picture the provision of forgiveness for sinners. As far as we know, this was the first time a living creature died by shedding of blood. Hebrews 9:22 specifies the Divine rule: "Without the shedding of blood, there is no remission of sin." Let the protestors clamor all they wish about "bloody religion", or "slaughterhouse theology", the wages of sin have not been reduced. Sin still causes death in its varying forms. The payment for sin must be of the exact kind and degree as the penalty for sin.

Third, there is in this picture a double type (a two-fold picture) of God's salvation. As a precautionary measure, let me repeat that this is a picture of a full New Testament reality. First, blood was shed to atone for sin. Second, a sufficient covering was "made" for Adam and Eve and placed on them by God Himself. Note again that every part of the necessary requirement was provided by God alone. This is the sinner's hope of Heaven. This is my only—but fully sufficient—hope of Heaven. Blood was shed as atonement for my sins, to save me from Hell, and a total covering of Perfect Righteousness, that of Jesus Christ, was provided to qualify me for Heaven. I can shout with Isaiah, "I will greatly rejoice in the LORD, my soul shall be joyful in my God; for He has clothed me with the garments of salvation, He has covered me with the robe of righteousness, as a bridegroom decks himself with ornaments, and as a bride adorns herself with her jewels" (Isaiah 61:10). As a person remaining temporarily in a condition of sinfulness, I am at one and the same time a perfectly-covered sinner and one of God's saints, the best-dressed folks in the universe!

This is the very heart of the Gospel of Christ. If you are one of those stubborn sinners who remains in your own "rags of (self-) righteousness", let me urge you to abandon hope in yourself. Such hope is vain, futile and fruitless, anyway. Then, in total self-distrust, cast yourself into the nail-pierced Hands of Christ, receive Him and the covering for your sins He has provided by His atoning Death on the Cross, and let Him clothe you in the *"fine linen, clean and white"* (Revelation 19:8) of His Righteousness. Then, you can enter Heaven without the disqualification of your sins, and with a qualification for Heaven that is equal to that of Christ Himself. Thus, you will be as acceptable in Heaven as if you *were Christ!*

*"Because the sinless Savior died, My sinful soul is counted free;*
*And God the Just is satisfied, To look on Him, and pardon Me!"*

Anyone who has not read Mark Twain's The Prince and the Pauper should make haste to correct the omission. I found the facetious and connived work to be considerably more than a very entertaining attempt by the famed American author to do some cross-cultural fantasy writing. Because of my happy Gospel bias, I found the little book to be an education in several Gospel realities, though I am certain this was not in the author's mind as he wrote. In summary, Tom Canty, a London pauper, through a similarity of appearance and a resulting mistake of identity, was received and royally treated at the Palace as if he were Edward, Prince of Wales, just as the believer in Christ, though a moral and spiritual pauper, is received in Heaven and royally treated as if he were Jesus, the Royal Crown Prince of the Realm! Just as Tom was "magnificently habited" in "purple cloth" and "white satin" for the reception, the believer in Jesus Christ is covered with the blood of Christ and His Perfect Righteousness. Mark Twain exclaimed on the page, "O Tom Canty, born in a hovel, bred in the gutters of London, familiar with rags and dirt and misery, what a spectacle is this!" This is an illustration of our Genesis type, a type of the justification and royal reception by God in the Courts of Heaven of believers in Christ.

In Jesus' most famous story, the same truth is presented in parable form. When the prodigal son returned home with the sins and stains of the far country evident upon his person, his loving, gracious father put the "best robe" in the household on him and covered over all the signs of his wandering. So does God graciously provide the covering of the Perfect Righteousness of Christ, as a robe woven on the looms of Heaven, to cover all of our sins. When David gratuitously placed crippled, cowardly, confused Mephibosheth at his own table in the King's palace, with his crippled legs out of sight under the bright white linen tablecloth, the derelict son of Saul was as accepted as if he were the King's only son! So does God graciously treat sinners when they come in the Name of His Only Son. Earlier in the life of David, he and Jonathan, as part of a covenant shared between them, exchanged apparel with one another. Even so, Jesus has "changed clothes" with us, taking the filthy rags of our sins and giving us instead the perfect robe of His pure righteousness. We are "accepted in the Beloved" (Ephesians 1:6)! This is God's Full, Final, Free Cure for the Fall of Man. As one old country preacher exclaimed, "Sinner, don't miss it if you can!"

# *AN ADDENDUM OF RELATED TRUTHS ON THE MISERY OF MAN*

"Wars may be fought on battlefields, but they are usually won or lost in the general's tent before the army goes to the battlefront." One of the first rules of warfare is, "Know your enemy." A wise General who knows he will soon lead his army into battle will study everything he can about the strategy and warfare tactics of the enemy. If we were a battalion of soldiers who were going into battle tomorrow, we would want to be involved in intense preparation today. Our commander would gather us together and tell us everything he knows about the enemy. He would brief us on his strategy. He would tell us how the enemy would attack and from which direction he would likely come. He would tell us what type of weapons the enemy would employ. And he would present a battle plan for defeating our foe. Strange, isn't it, when the church is engaged in a war how few leaders ever mention the enemy to the troops, much less instruct them about the battle. Is it any wonder so many Christians are defeated? It is hard to win a war if we do not know where or how or against whom it is being fought.

Just yesterday, an "email friend" sent me a story which I wish to adapt as an illustration of Satan's temptation-procedure. "A foreign exchange student was in a Chemistry class in a large college. In a private moment, the student asked the professor this strange question: 'Do you know how to catch wild pigs?' Thinking it was a joke, the professor asked for the punch line. 'This is not a joke,' the young student answered, and proceeded to explain the procedure he knew for catching wild pigs. 'You catch wild pigs by finding a suitable place in the woods and putting corn on the ground. The pigs find it and begin to come every day to eat the free corn. When they are used to coming every day, you put a fence down one side of the place where they are used to coming. When they get used to the fence, they begin to eat the corn again and you put up another side of the fence. They get used to that and start to eat again. You continue until you have all four sides of the fence up with a gate in the last side. The pigs that are used to the free corn start to come through the gate to eat, and then you slam the gate on them and catch the whole herd. Suddenly the wild pigs have lost their freedom. They run around inside the fence, but they are caught. Soon they go back to eating the free corn. They are so used to it that they have forgotten how to forage in the woods for themselves, so they accept their captivity.'"

Friends, this is an overt illustration of the covert strategy Satan followed in snaring Eve. Once she was captured, he left the matter in her hands, and she, fully snared, offered the bait to Adam and he was snared, too! I remember as a boy often hearing these lines of enticement, usually when someone was holding a sweet candy in his/her hand and offering it to me:

>*"Open your mouth and shut your eyes;*
>*I'll give you something to make you wise."*

I am quite sure that poem of enticement is an echo of the Garden of Eden exchange from Eve to Adam. What was Satan's subtle strategy? First, Satan penetrated Eve's mind with a mild suggestion of doubt. Then he stimulated a selfish desire in her heart. Then, he secured the sinful decision from her that he hoped for: "She did eat" (Genesis 3:6). First, one fence was put up to trap her, but it looked innocent enough—she was still free. But then a second was erected, enclosing more of her mind in agreement with him. Then a third fence, and finally, she was captive to sin and could not turn back. You see, this story is not merely an old crusty myth stored in the dusty archives of ancient "religious" history. It is as up-to-date as today's newspaper—in fact, the full dimensions of this temptation story can be easily traced in today's news, and the final dimensions of this story can be regularly seen in the headlines of the daily newspaper, and in the "breaking news" of today's telecasts.

Look at the steady but stealthy assault that Satan made on Eve's mind. Wrong thinking is usually the basis for wrong doing. A mere insinuation led Eve to debate that which should not even have been considered. When she started to dialogue with the Devil at his lead, she was lost. When the Devil tempted Jesus in the wilderness, the Master did not discuss the matter from Satan's point of view. Instead, a quick, sharp, ringing reply of refusal came from the Divine side. You see, the human mind is like a hotel or motel. The manager of the establishment can't keep people in the lobby from asking for a room, but he can certainly keep them from getting one. Martin Luther paraphrased this truth in these words, "You may not be able to keep a bird from flying over your head, but you can keep it from building a nest in your hair!" It is too late to return to Eden (read Genesis 3:24), so man uneasily roams around inside the fences of his captivity, a slave of sin but not wanting to admit it. Also, the pain is alleviated temporarily (though it comes back with more intensity later) by the fact that there is plenty of "free corn" inside the fences. But all of it is "outside of Eden."

*Chapter 6*

# THE MEASURE OF MAN

*"We dare not make ourselves of the number, or compare ourselves with some that commend themselves; but they measuring themselves by themselves, and comparing themselves among themselves, are not wise"* (II Corinthians 10:12)

*"Not he that commendeth himself is approved, but whom the Lord commendeth"* (II Corinthians 10:17-18)

*"We shall all be judged one day, not by each other's standard, or even by our own, but by the standard of Christ"* (Romans 14:10, Phillips paraphrase)

*"God has fixed a day on which He will judge the whole world in justice by the standard of a Man whom He has appointed. He has guaranteed to all men that this is so by raising This Man from the dead"* (Acts 17:31, Phillips paraphrase)

The description which Paul gives of some of the church members at Corinth is so timely today that it is almost frightening. The practice he mentions is just as common and destructive today as it was when he wrote about it. It is the practice of men measuring themselves by inferior standards of life and living.

Every serious basketball fan is familiar with the name of Bobby Knight, head coach at the University of Indiana. When Knight was in Louisiana, he saw a bolt of red cloth that he thought would make a great Indiana University jacket. He bought the cloth, took it to his tailor in Bloomington, and asked him to make a jacket. The tailor said, "Coach, there's not enough cloth here for me to make a jacket for you." Bobby Knight was disappointed, but he put the cloth into the back seat of his car. Several weeks later, he was in Lexington, Kentucky, on a recruiting trip, and he saw a tailor's shop there. He took the cloth into the shop and asked the tailor, "Could you make me a jacket out of this cloth?" The tailor in Lexington said, "Sure. I can make you a jacket, a pair of trousers, and a vest out of that cloth." Bobby Knight said, "My tailor in Indiana told me there wasn't enough cloth here even to make a jacket. How can you do all that?" The tailor replied, "There's one thing you've got to understand, Coach. You're just not as big down here in Kentucky as you are up there in Indiana!" You see, there are standards of measurement, and then there are *standards of measurement.*

Every life needs a perfect yardstick — an unchangeable standard by which it can be regularly measured. And it must be remembered that a yard is always 36 inches, not 22 or even 32.

How do you measure yourself? This is one of the most important questions you will face--in time and in eternity. We are all measuring ourselves by one standard or another every day of our lives. And we shall be satisfied with pygmy stature unless we use standard measuring-sticks. John Henry Jowett said, "The value of anyone's judgments depends absolutely upon the quality of his standards of judgment. If the standard is poor, the judgment is altogether worthless." How we measure up depends on what the measure is.

The verses of our text present the only three standards by which you may measure yourself. Those standards are: The *Personal* standard, the *Public* standard, and the *Perfect* standard. Or, to word it differently, I may measure myself by *Myself*, by the *Masses*, or by the *Master*. Let's examine these three standards of measurement.

## I. The Individual Standard of Self-Measurement

First, you can measure yourself by an *individual* standard, the standard of individual comparison. *You can measure yourself by yourself.* In Romans 14:10 (Phillips' translation), the Bible says that we can measure ourselves "by our own" standard. In II Corinthians 10:12, Paul says, "They, measuring themselves by themselves...are not wise."

It is possible for you to measure yourself by a standard of your own devising. In this case, you simply set your own standard — for moral conduct, for social behavior, and for ethical practice in business or profession. You pay no attention to any objective ideals. If you want green to be yellow and purple to be pink, you just declare them to be so, and that settles it. You are your own standard of judgment. You are absolute and almighty as the god of your own world — or so you think. Whatever you say goes. You see, I can run a two-minute mile — if you will let *me* decide how long a mile is (or, how long a *minute* is). I can jump twenty feet in the air — if you will let *me* decide how long a foot is. Ridiculous, isn't it? Remember, how we measure up depends on what the measure is.

The Bible says, "They, measuring themselves by themselves, are not wise." One social commentator said, "Self-commenders live in a paradise of fools." But every man likes to flatter himself. Many are like the little boy who told his mother that he was nine feet tall. But, when she investigated she discovered that he was measuring himself, not by a twelve-inch standard foot, but by the length of his own shoe.

A man was driving through a rural Kentucky community. Everywhere he looked, he saw bull's-eye targets painted on the sides of barns, stores, and walls. Each target had a bullet hole exactly in the middle of it. He stopped at a store and asked who the expert rifleman, the marksman, was. The reply was, "Oh, that's the village simpleton. He fires the bullet into the wall, and then draws the bull's-eye around the bullet hole!" The Way translation of II Corinthians 10:12 says, "Some stand sponsors for themselves: They measure their own worth by a standard of their own."

Actually, the person who measures himself by his own standard is reproducing the sin of Adam and Eve all over again, seeking to be "the whole cheese" in his own world. But we must remind ourselves of the endless and chaotic consequences of their action in the Garden of Eden. If we want to run the risk of total anarchy and its horrible consequences in this world, and eternal judgment and damnation in the next, we can measure ourselves by our own standards.

## II. The Interpersonal Standard of Society's Measurement

Second, you can measure yourself by an *interpersonal* standard, the standard of interpersonal comparison. *You can measure yourself by other people.* In Romans 14:10 (Phillips translation), the Bible speaks of those who "measure themselves... by comparisons within their own circle." And in II Corinthians 10:12, Paul says, "Comparing themselves among themselves, they are not wise."

However, there is an impulse to *compare* — and to *compete* — in every human heart. It was comedian George Carlin who said, "Just drive out onto the freeway — and listen to yourself think (and you may not have to listen intently, because you *may* be thinking *out loud*). Everyone who drives *faster* than you is an *idiot,* and everyone who drives *slower* than you is a *moron.*" Carlin's words should enable us to see that the tendency to compare and compete opens the door to many problems and many sins. To practice comparison with other human beings is usually to be trapped into sin. If they are not as virtuous as we are, we slip into spiritual pride. If they are more virtuous than we are, we fall into feelings of envy, inferiority, or despair. In the first case, we lower our own level by the sin of comparison, and in the second case, we may try to lower the other person's virtue with jealous accusations and charges.

I suppose that our greatest skill in measuring ourselves lies at this point — and our greatest problem. Which one of us has never thought to himself, "Well, I guess I'm doing pretty well. I'm just as good as others and a lot better than some." And we follow up on this analysis by nearly breaking our arm to pat ourselves on the back. It seems that comparing ourselves with our neighbors who are as imperfect as we are has a way of convincing us of our moral and spiritual goodness, even our superiority. An old cliché says, "In the country of the blind, a one-eyed man is king." If we can suppose that we have at least one eye while everybody else is blind, we can imagine our own royalty. But another cliché provides balance: "You can't clear your own field while counting the rocks on your neighbor's farm."

Two animals met one day out on the road of life. Both animals were blind. One was a rabbit and the other was a snake. When each discerned the other's plight, one said to the other, "We must help each other know what we are. Why don't we feel of each other, describe what we feel, and then we can decide what we are." The snake said, "I'll examine you first." The snake began to feel of the rabbit's body. "You're covered with soft fur all over. You have four legs, and the two back legs stay curled up when you're sitting still. You have a curved back. You have a soft, wet, twitching nose, two soft round eyes, and two long, floppy ears." The rabbit shouted, "Hallelujah! I know what I am! I'm a rabbit!" And the rabbit jumped around in happy celebration. The snake stopped the celebration with the words, "Now you must help me find out what I am." So the rabbit began to feel the body of the snake. "You have a hard triangular head, and long, thin, beady eyes. You are crooked all the way through, and you have diamonds all over your body." The snake shouted, "Hallelujah! I know what I am! I'm a television evangelist!" Our comparisons of ourselves with others may lead to an equally comical, or blind, evaluation.

Two brothers were notoriously immoral. When one of them died, the surviving brother, trying to maintain a semblance of respectability, went to the local pastor and requested him to perform the funeral service. He even offered the pastor a great sum of money if, in his eulogy, he would refer to the deceased brother as a saint. After much thought, the pastor agreed. In his eulogy, the pastor said, "The man we have come to bury was a thief. In fact, he deserves the worst description the mind can muster. He was depraved, immoral, obscene, hateful, vicious, and licentious. He was the filth of the earth. But compared to his brother, he was a saint!" You see, one of the most deceptive aspects of our sinfulness is often the twisted tendency to justify ourselves by comparison to some other person.

Those who live by comparison easily fall prey to some very ugly sins — envy, jealousy, dishonesty, hypocrisy, deceit. They become like the young lady applying for a job. The personnel director said, "These are some very good references you have here." She responded, "Well, thank you. I wrote them myself!"

Hal Luccock told of a little girl whose mother found her crying because a poor family down the street had moved away. "I didn't know you cared so much for those children," the mother said. But the little girl's answer explained the real problem when she said, "Now there's nobody in the neighborhood that I am better than." In order to find someone we're "better than", we use measures of our own making.

The Apostle Paul declared that this practice of interpersonal comparisons "doesn't make sense." He declared that anyone who does it is "not wise." Unless you are the most deficient person in the world morally and spiritually, it is always easy to find someone near you, against whom you shape up pretty well. That is probably the reason why some of us choose certain people for associates. It is a comfort to have someone beside us over whom we feel superior. We are experts at forcing comparisons.

Some boys were playing football near a chicken yard. Accidentally their white football was kicked into the chicken yard where the rooster and about twenty hens were feeding. The rooster examined the big white egg, then he called the hens over and said, "Now, girls, I'm not trying to intimidate you, but I want you to see what the hens next door are producing!" Paul was right. It "doesn't make sense."

A man was the timekeeper in a cotton mill. On his way to work every day, he stopped by a jeweler's shop and checked his watch by the clock in the shop window. One day the jeweler was standing outside the shop when the mill worker came by. He said to him, "I see you always check your watch by my clock. You come every day." And with a smile, he added, "You're as faithful as clock-work." The mill worker replied, "Yes, I check my watch every day. You see, I work down at the cotton mill, and my job is to blow the whistle at the beginning and end of each shift. I want to be sure my time is right, so every day I check my watch with you." "That's funny!" replied the jeweler, "I set my clock every day by your whistle!" This is the situation that exists when we take our standards from one another. We think something is right because we do it; and we may be doing something that is altogether wrong. The Phillips' translation of II Corinthians 10:12 says, Measuring by one another "doesn't make for accurate estimation, you may be sure." When we take our standards from each other, the trend can only be downwards, because of our sinful, fallen human nature.

The Bible says, "There is a generation pure in their own eyes, yet they are not washed from their filth" (Proverbs 30:12). Note the stark contrast between the two words of assessment, "pure" and "filthy." The word "filthy" is the Holy Spirit's assessment of this generation, the accurate one, while the word "pure" is the self-assessment of the people of this generation, the false evaluation. Could it be that the Holy Spirit and the people of this generation measure men by two very different standards of measurement?

Several years ago, in his column in the New York Herald Tribune, Hy Gardner told the interesting (and enlightening) story of a counterfeiter named "Blinky". It seems that Blinky felt that he had achieved a perfect copy of a $10 bill. In spite of his slick production he was arrested by a United States treasury agent. Feeling boldly confident about his foolproof engravings, Blinky boasted, "I don't believe you can tell me the difference between the two bills." To Blinky's astonishment, the agent replied, "That's just the point, Blinky. There is no difference. Seems you only made one mistake. You copied your counterfeit from a counterfeit!" He copied an exact likeness, but he used an inferior standard. And many of us are doing the same thing.

Look at the many cases of unwise comparison in the Bible. In the earliest story of sinful comparison in the Bible (Genesis 4), Cain could not bear the success of the offering of his brother Abel — so he murdered him! In the parable of the Pharisee and publican in the Temple, they both went to church on the same day. The Pharisee despised the publican by assuming a high stance of superiority over him, thanking God that he was not "like this publican." But Jesus said that he went away from church far worse, not better, than when he went. In the renowned "parable of the prodigal son," the elder brother clearly saw his brother's mistakes, but because he compared himself with him, he was blinded to his own self-righteousness. In another parable, a debtor who owed an unpayable debt nonetheless saw himself as far superior to a man who owed him only a small debt. In yet another parable, the laborers who had earned their day's wages thought themselves much finer men than those who were paid without earning it.

Simon Peter had just had a life-transforming encounter with Jesus (John 21) when the text says that he "turned and saw that other disciple whom Jesus loved follow them. When Peter saw him, he asked, 'Lord, what about him?' Jesus answered, 'What is that to you? You follow me.'" Notice that Peter was less concerned about the seriousness of his own fate than with how it would compare with John's fate. Note, also, that Jesus did not tell Peter that all the stresses and strains would balance out. He did not say that because He is perfect love and perfect justice, each of His children would have equal experience. Jesus said, in effect, "What happens to John is none of your affair. You yourself are to follow my personal plan for your individual life. Peter, you are to follow me, even to martyrdom, if that is where I lead you." In other words, "Don't make a comparison between John and yourself. The real comparison to make is between what I command you (follow Me, and feed My sheep) and what you do in response to My command." The fact is that we too easily stick our noses into the lives of other Christians, concentrating on their successes, feats, fame, fortunes, and fates, and thus we slip in neglecting the clear directions Jesus has given us.

One of my favorite authors is C. S. Lewis. His <u>Chronicles of Narnia</u> are favorites of mine. Jesus is forever showing up through some aspect of his stories. There is a passage in Lewis' <u>The Horse and His Boy</u> which powerfully illustrates our point. The boy, Shasta, is conversing with the Christ figure of the story, the lion named Aslan. Aslan is recounting his sovereign workings in Shasta's life, that he was the lion who drove the jackals away while Shasta slept, and comforted him among the houses of the dead, and propelled the boat which bore him to the shore to receive help. As Shasta listened, reflecting on the lion's sovereign claims, he suddenly asked, "Then it was you who wounded Aravis?" "It was I." "But what for?" "Child," said the Voice, "I am telling your story, not hers. I tell no one any story but his own." Dear Christian, we must let our personal stories be developed by a close and qualitative walk with Jesus that absorbs all of our concerns, and we must let Him work out His purposes in His other children, lending our assistance without the necessity of worthless and sinful comparisons.

Let's reduce it to personal terms — as, indeed, we do every day. Suppose I come to you, and I say, "Among all the noble characters in the Bible, whom shall I take as my moral model?" After a moment of thought, you reply, "Why don't you try Abraham? He is a good example for you." Thinking out loud, I answer, "Abraham. That sounds like a good suggestion. He was a great man, a friend of God and father of the faithful. But, wait a minute! If I adopt him as my moral standard, do you want me to lie as Abraham lied!" You see, Abraham (as great as he was) is not fit to be my example. You way, "Well, then, how about Moses?" "Moses! Well, he certainly was a magnificent man, one of the greatest in world history — an historian, a statesman, a legislator. But, hold on! Do you want me to violently lose my temper as Moses lost his temper? Or commit murder as he did?" Moses (as great as he was) is not worthy to be my moral pattern. Perhaps a little less confidently now, you say, "How about David?" "David," I answer, "To be sure, he was a splendid personality--a warrior, a poet, a man after God's own heart. But I ask you, do you want me to commit adultery--and murder, as David committed adultery and murder?" You see, by the simple process of elimination, we can pass through history and show that there is only One Person of all that have been born of woman who is perfectly fit to be the Model, the Pattern, and the Example for us to measure ourselves by.

Jesus, our Savior and Model, left the eternal glory of the Father to suffer the ultimate humiliation of a shameful human death. Yet, He never complained because He had to abandon the glory that the other two members of the Trinity retained. If He had compared His role in redemption with those of the Father and the Holy Spirit, He might have felt cheated. Why should He — equal with the other two — be the One to become the scum of the earth? What if He had said, "I'm just not into crosses!"

If Jesus had compared Himself with *other men,* He might have thought that He should be the greatest of men. Yet (incredibly) He became the lowest of them! When the disciples were wondering who would perform the duties of a household servant, Christ took a towel and a basin of water and washed their feet! Jesus did not compare Himself with others, but cared only about meeting the standard that the Father had ordained. That was all that mattered.

Author Dennis McCallum, in his book, <u>Walking in Victory</u>, has a lengthy illustration that registers this point: Suppose that nothing existed in the universe except you. There you are, floating in a bubble in the midst of infinite, empty space. What would your identity be? What would you consider important? Suppose you asked yourself, "Am I tall or short?" "Hmm," you say, "Tall or short compared to whom?" Ideas like tall and short come from comparisons with others. But nothing and no one exists in this imaginary universe but you. Would you consider yourself smart or stupid? Here again, these concepts are directly dependent on perceptions of yourself relative to others. If you were the only one in the universe, such concepts would be meaningless. And so it would go in every area. Whether it concerned things you did, features you found in yourself, or whatever, there would be no way to assign importance to these things.

Consequently, you would have no sense of identity. You could only wonder who you were and whether you mattered, how you got there and where you were going; you could never know. Suppose in your lonely universe another person suddenly appears, also floating in a bubble. At least now you have someone to compare yourself to. We could call this person an external reference point, because he or she isn't inside your head. You might notice you are taller than the other person and thus conclude that you are a tall person. However, for all you know, this other person might be the littlest midget ever, and you wouldn't be very tall, after all. Since both of you are floating in a sea of infinite nothingness, your comparisons would all be of questionable importance. You might notice that you have five fingers, but the other person in the universe has six. Is this important? Or just a curiosity? There is no way to tell. You now have an external point of reference, a reference point outside yourself. The problem is, this external reference point is, like yourself, finite, or limited. There is no reason to think the other person's features are better or more authoritative than your own.

Therefore, there is no way to tell what the real story is. Are you tall, or is the other person short? In such a universe, everything would be relative; nothing in the area of values would be certain. Apart from God, the human race is living in this dilemma. Instead of one other person to compare ourselves with, we have millions. This means we can begin to establish sociological averages, but nothing more. When we draw the camera back, we will realize that, although we as individuals are not floating alone in space without meaning, our whole planet is floating in space; so what's the difference? All the people on our planet decide somehow which comparisons are important and which are not. But if there is no absolute perspective to which we can relate our judgments, they are all quite arbitrary. But what if there were an absolute, or ultimate, ruler by which we could measure things? According to the biblical view, there is such an absolute. God is a reference point, but He is different from the finite reference point in our earlier illustration. Because He is infinite and unlimited, He is also universal, or absolute, rather than relative. Other things can be related to God, but He doesn't need to relate to anyone or anything to know who He is. If we believe the Bible, we should realize that God's view of us is the true view, and that if He views us a certain way, then that is, in the ultimate sense, the way we really are!

It would be well to go back and read that long section again. It both shows the inadequacy and the folly of our attempts at comparison with each other. But it also introduces another possibility, which becomes a necessity if we are to live life as it was intended. You can measure yourself "by comparisons within your own circle," or "by the standards set by others," but if you do, rest assured that your final testimony will be like that of King Saul in the Old Testament, who said, "I have played the fool."

## III. The Ideal Standard of the Savior's Measurement

There is one other possible standard of comparison. You can, and should, measure yourself by the *ideal* standard, the standard of ideal comparison. You can (and should) measure yourself by the perfect and unchanging standard of Jesus Christ. Romans 14:10 (Phillips translation) says, "We shall all be judged one day...by the standard of Jesus Christ." Acts 17:31 echoes the same truth: "God has fixed a day on which He will judge the whole world in justice by the standard of a Man whom He has appointed. He has guaranteed to all men that this is so by raising This Man from the dead." Thus, we have a standard of measurement by which we will be tested — and furthermore, we need such a standard!

When John Quincy Adams was President of the United States, he called both Houses of Congress together for a special meeting. He walked upon the rostrum carrying two bushel measures. Holding one in each hand, he said to the audience, "The bushel measure in my right hand came from South Carolina; the one in my left hand comes from the city of New York. One of these bushel measures contains sixty-eight cubic inches more than the other one." He stood silent for a few moments to let the implication sink in; then he slowly placed them side by side on the floor. In the same deliberate way, he walked over to a little table and picked up two one-pound weights, the kind that were used on a set of balance scales to weigh produce. With measured words he said, "This weight in my right hand came from Massachusetts; this other one came from Maine. One of them weighs nearly an ounce more than the other." Again he waited a few moments for everyone to grasp the problem. Then with a resonant voice he said, "Gentlemen, we need a standard measure and a standard weight for the United States of America." Thus came into existence the United States Bureau of Weights and Measures. The necessity created the reality.

Are arbitrariness and anarchy to characterize man? Those who so militantly seek the "freedom" to do as they please will not finally be pleased with what they are *forced* to do. Though it is a tough challenge to man's vain autonomy, man needs a standard of measurement that is totally independent of him. We have standards for measuring everything. We measure weight in terms of ounces, pounds, and tons. We measure distance in terms of inches, feet, yards, and miles. We measure time in terms of seconds, minutes, hours, days, months, years, decades, and centuries. We have standards for measuring nearly everything. God, also, has His standard for measuring us, and that standard is Jesus Christ. In Ephesians 4:13, we find this phrase: "The measure of the stature of the fullness of Christ." This is the measure by which God measures us! And this is the only true standard by which we should measure ourselves.

When I was fourteen years of age, I moved with my parents to a location only two blocks from the campus of the University of Arkansas in Fayetteville. For four years, I observed student painters from art classes station themselves all over the terrain surrounding the campus to paint all imaginable objects — trees, walls, buildings, railroad scenes, sky and clouds, people, landscapes, etc. It seemed peculiar to me that they even went out in the coldest winter, when the ground was covered with snow, and sat for one or two hours at a sitting. I wondered why the students didn't take a photograph of the scene and paint from it. When I entered college, I received an explanation. A young art student said, "We are taught not to paint from a photograph or any other copy, but to paint only while looking at the original." Paint only while looking at the original! This is the only sensible thing for a human being to do.

Blaise Pascal, the great French mathematician, scientist, and philosopher, said he envisioned his Lord saying to him, "Do not compare yourself with others, but with Me. If you do not find Me in the one with whom you compare yourself, you are comparing yourself with one who is abominable. If you do find Me in the one with whom you compare yourself, then why not compare yourself with Me?" Henry Drummond said, "For more than twenty-five years, I instinctively have gone to Christ to draw a measure and a rule for everything." The Holy Spirit calls him "wise"!

However, no sooner does the wise man draw a comparison between himself and Jesus than *he finds himself greatly embarrassed*. There is no way a sinful human being can initially be comfortable when measuring himself by the perfect standard of Jesus Christ.

A tourist was enjoying the Louvre Art Gallery in Paris. He overheard another tourist ask the guard why the large wastebaskets were set at the door of the gallery. The guard replied, "This is where the young artists drop their conceits when they go out." Asked to explain, he replied, "These youngsters come in here convinced they're on the way to being great artists. But after comparing their sketches with the paintings of the masters, they, now thoroughly chastised for their arrogance, discard their pitiful attempts in the wastebasket on the way out." The same experience often happens in men's souls. Comparing ourselves with ourselves or our neighbors who are as imperfect as we are may deceive us into avowing our own moral and spiritual goodness. However, when we place our poor lives alongside that of our perfect Master, our radical sin and inadequacy are seen. A match may flare brightly when lit in a dark room, but the same burning match fades into insignificance when exposed to the light of the sun.

Several years ago, <u>Peloubet's Notes</u> related the following incident: Those who wished to qualify for positions in the elite guard of King

Frederick of Prussia were required to measure up to a certain commanding stature. A Christian lady thought so much about this annual "Measuring Day" ceremony that when she went to bed one evening she had a dream in which she imagined there was a day when everyone's growth in *grace* was similarly measured. An angel stood with a long golden rod in his hand over which was fastened a scroll on which appeared these words: "The measure of the stature of the perfect man." The angel inscribed in a large book all the important statistics as the people came up one at a time in response to the calling of their names. The instant anyone touched the rod an astounding thing appeared — each shrank or increased in size to his or her true *spiritual dimensions*! Everyone, including the recording angel, could thus miraculously see what otherwise would have been perceived only by the eye of God.

If today — *today* — were the "Measuring Day," would you be ashamed of your spiritual stature? A man who is only four feet six inches tall does not need to be told that he is a dwarf when standing next to a man of six feet four inches. He knows it--just by standing there and looking! And when my stunted life is set over against the towering standard of Jesus Christ, I do not have to be told that I am missing the moral mark and have "fallen short of the glory of God." I know it — just by standing there and looking at Him!

I would be very cautious here. I don't want to leave the impression that measuring yourself by Jesus is an *option* in life. It isn't; it is an *obligation*. It isn't *elective*; it is absolutely *essential*. The text says, "We shall all be judged one day...by the standard of Jesus Christ." Many people try to keep their distance from Jesus because they are intimidated by the perfection of His Life and embarrassed by the vision they see of themselves when they get close to Him. So, to prevent this embarrassment, they avoid any contact that might produce this embarrassment. In fact, many, many people even stay away from church for this very reason! But how utterly unwise this is! The Bible plainly says, "God has fixed a day in which he will judge the whole world in justice by the standard of the man whom he has appointed, Jesus Christ" (Acts 17:31). And yet, folly of follies, when I measure myself by Jesus Christ, the Perfect Pattern, the Moral Model for all men, I am horrified by the reality that I do not "measure up" at any point of comparison. Is God only mocking me? Not at all! God is merely making me aware of my absolute need of a Savior. And wonder of wonders, Jesus Christ, who is the standard of measurement for my sinful life, also offers Himself to me as my Savior from sin. You see, He perfectly loves me in spite of my sins, and came to the earth to die for me and my sins. Friend, He died personally for you as if you were the only sinner who ever needed to be died for. If you will confess your sins directly to Him, throw yourself on the mercy of God's court, and trust Him as your own Savior, He will save you in a moment. To trust Him is to receive Him in all His fullness into your life. In the very moment that any sinner trusts Jesus Christ, God credits the perfect righteousness of Jesus (all that Jesus is and has done) to that sinner's account so that He does not see his sins anymore, but He sees instead the perfect purity of Jesus credited to his account. So the very purity of Christ which threatens the sinner as a measurement for his life, now covers him to make him presentable to God! No wonder this message is called "the Gospel," or "Good News!"

Dr. L. Nelson Bell, who was for many years a missionary to China, shares this wonderful illustration: "The Chinese word for 'righteousness' is the Chinese character that means 'lamb' set above the Chinese character for the personal pronoun 'me' — a marvelous illustration of the fact that when God looks upon a person who believes in His Son, the Lamb of God, and receives Him into His heart, God sees, from that moment on, not the person's sin, but the righteousness of Christ covering him and standing to his credit — forever!" THE LAMB OVER ME! HALLELUJAH!

Have you trusted Jesus Christ as your own Savior and Lord? Either you must receive His mercy or you will be measured by Him and judged by your failure to meet His standard. Either you must take Christ or take the consequences. I urge you to repent of your sins, trust Christ to save you, receive Him into your heart by faith, and rest in Him today and every day. This is how you "measure up" in God's eyes.

*Chapter 7*

# MERCY FOR MAN

*"The sin of Judah is written with a pen of iron, and with the point of a diamond: it is graven upon the table of their heart, and upon the horns of your altars. . . . The heart is deceitful above all things, and desperately wicked: who can know it?" (Jeremiah 17:1, 9)*

*"And you, being dead in your sins and the uncircumcision of your flesh, hath he quickened together with him, having forgiven you all trespasses; Blotting out the handwriting of ordinances that was against us, which was contrary to us, and took it out of the way, nailing it to his cross; And having spoiled principalities and powers, he made a show of them openly, triumphing over them in it." (Colossians 2:13-15)*

*"Do we begin again to commend ourselves? Or need we, as some others, epistles of commendation to you, or letters of commendation from you? Ye are our epistle written in our hearts, known and read of all men: Forasmuch as ye are manifestly declared to be the epistles of Christ ministered by us, written not with ink, but with the Spirit of the living God; not in tables of stone, but in fleshly tables of the heart." (II Corinthians 3:1-3)*

These three passages of Scripture are far apart in your Bible, but they are drawn together by the fact that they all deal with substantially the same metaphor or illustration. They all have to do with something written, something recorded, a message indelibly inscribed. In the first and last texts, the thing written is inscribed on the human heart; in the middle text, the thing recorded is written in God's record books, and it stands against man until God deals with it. The first and second text have to do with the record of sin, and the last text has to do with what the Holy Spirit is writing on the Christian's heart once the record of sin is removed. So the entire drama of *sin, salvation, sanctification* and *service* is traced colorfully in these three passages. Sin is the primary theme of the first passage, salvation is the main theme of the second passage, and sanctification and service are the big ideas that dominate the third passage. May we trust the Holy Spirit to teach us as we explore these three passages.

I have entitled this chapter, "Mercy Rewrote My Life," because this is the story of an original writing, an erasure of that original writing, and a rewriting on the erased page — with the last two being *miracles* accomplished by the marvelous mercy and grace of God.

## I. The Record of Sin in Human Experience

The first text suggests the deeply inscribed *record of sin* in human experience. According to the first text, sin is indelibly written (in the human heart — and in heaven) as a testimony against man. Jeremiah 17:1 contains a powerful witness of this record. It says, "The sin of Judah is written with a pen of iron, and with the point of a diamond: it is graven upon the table of their heart, and upon the horns of your altars." The symbolism is evident. An iron pen leaves deep indentations upon a clay tablet, and a diamond cuts deeply into a pane of glass. Even so sin itself not only leaves marks and scars in human character, but once it is committed, it is indelibly recorded.

Note the two places where the recording is made. One is "upon the table of their heart," and the other is "upon the horns of your altars." This means that the record of sin is deeply imbedded in the human character, and that it also stands as a public testimony between each man and God. It even stains any religion that the man may practice.

Here we see the fathomless *depth* of sin in human experience. Sin runs much deeper and much wider in human experience than the unaided person normally takes into account. The record of sin is recorded within an individual like a tattoo inscribed on the heart. It is so deeply ingrained there that it cannot be humanly erased, and must not be ignored. <u>The Rubaiyat of Omar Khayyam</u>, the ancient book of Persian wisdom, records this truth in these words:

> "The Moving Finger writes: And having writ,
> Moves on, And not all your piety nor wit
> Shall lure it back, to cancel half a line.
> And not all your tears can wash out a word of it."

When Bishop Hugh Latimer, the great English martyr, was on trial for his life, a trial which ended in his being burned at the stake, he at first freely answered all questions that were asked at the trial without giving any consideration to how much a single unguarded word might cost him. But one day while the trial was proceeding and he was giving his full and unchecked answers, he paused to think before continuing, when suddenly he heard the scratching pen of a recording secretary, who was seated behind a curtain taking down every expression which fell from his lips. From that point on, he tried to be more cautious with his words, but by then the damage had been done.

It would be wise for every unsaved human being to remember that there is a pen now recording our every evil deed and word and thought within our character and behind the curtain of the skies, and that for all these things God will bring us into judgment. The iron pen and the diamond point do not wear out. There is a secretary within you and a Secretary above you keeping an infallible record of your sins. Conscience is the secretary within, and the Holy Spirit is the Secretary above, and they are deeply and indelibly recording your sins. A record is also being kept of a believer's life—but that is another matter altogether—a Family matter.

Think of the record of sin written by the human conscience. Every man is perpetually writing a permanent record of himself. It is almost impossible for the average man to realize that the actions of each fast-moving moment of his life leave an indelible record, but it is true. These actions seem to fade quickly and completely out of existence once they are done, but this impression is false. The record of our past often seems to be written in water, but this is not so. When I was a young boy (back before the Dead Sea got sick!), we wrote messages on paper with "invisible ink." The messages could not be seen when they were written. However, one could take a candle or a burning match and hold it beneath the paper at a later time, and the "invisible" writing would come to visibility. So it is with every act, word, and thought of our past.

The Greek language has a perfect tense in its verb forms, and Greek grammarians define it as that tense which expresses an action completed in the past and having consequences that remain in the present and even in the indefinite future. That is true of all of our actions! Though they have been completed in the past, and seem to be buried away in the tomb of time, they are all permanent. Every day we are making entries in the diaries of our lives.

There is probably not a man alive who has not wished that some particular action of his past had not been done. He probably has said in some moment of sad reflection, "I would give anything if I had not done or said that." But it simply cannot be changed. Remorse cannot alter it. Wishes are futile. Even repentance cannot change the history of the sin committed. Reformation in the present and the future will not rewrite the indelible record of the past. The action committed at any moment is like the making of footprints in wet cement — it hardens immediately into unalterable history. We cannot influence an action once taken; we are at the mercy of that action from that point on — unless something acts upon the record to neutralize or negate it. The future is *potential*, but the past is *indelible*. Friend, are you satisfied with what you have written?

Some years ago, I read the life story of the late Peter Marshall, written by his wife, Catherine Marshall. In her book, entitled <u>A Man Called Peter</u>, Mrs. Marshall relates an illustration which Peter Marshall often told. It was about a rambunctious and mischievous little boy who packed a lot of havoc in one "creative" day. First, he squeezed all the toothpaste out of every tube of toothpaste in the bathrooms of his home (and even squeezed some of it in neat, zebra-like stripes across the back of the dozing house cat). Then he climbed his neighbor's apple trees and pulled all the apples from the trees. Later the same day, he walked by the barber shop where he had been forced to sit, restless and squirming, while the barber cut his hair. On this day, the barber had no customers, and so he had climbed into his own barbershop chair and had gone to sleep. When the boy saw this tempting situation his creativity overwhelmed him, and he slipped into the shop, took the barber's scissors, and systematically clipped off all of the barber's hair he thought he could cut, and still not be caught. Well, of course, he was caught and his misdeeds were exposed. As a part of his punishment, his father issued a peculiar command. "Son," he said, "you will put all the toothpaste back into the tubes, put all the apples back on the trees, and attach all the hair which you cut back onto the barber's head." What was his point? The point is that once a thing is done, it cannot be undone. Once a sin is committed, it cannot be uncommitted. The message of the text is that the committed sin is also a recorded sin, and the depth of its record is of such a nature that only God's grace can eradicate it.

We see in the other text from Jeremiah seventeen the deceitfulness of sin. Verse nine says, "For the heart is deceitful above all things, and desperately wicked; who can know it?" This verse only declares what becomes evident about the human heart when it is carefully examined. Fill a container with dirty or muddy water and the sediment will gradually -- and visibly -- settle to the bottom. The water will appear cleaner and purer. However, the slightest motion will stir the sediment and bring it surging to the top again. The water will become thick and murky as before. This is a picture of the sinful human heart. The heart is full of the sediment of dirty sin, and thus no pure life can naturally flow from it. However, many a person is deceived at this point, because sometimes the dirt is at rest, and sinks to the bottom. But then let an occasion or opportunity to sin occur, and the heart will be stirred to show its impurity again. Evangelist D. L. Moody often said, "If a photographer came through the community who could photograph the moral condition of the human heart, he would starve to death before he could get a customer. You would not want all the horrible truth of your heart shown for public examination, would you?"

Is there a solution? Yes, but it is found only in the cleansing of the Blood of Christ and the continuous flow of the Water of Life through the believer's heart. The Blood of Christ cleanses away the contamination of sin, and the Water of Life continues to replace it with the Life of God.

The Hebrew word translated "deceitful" is from the verb *ya'qob*, which is related to the familiar name of the Old Testament character, Jacob. Though Jacob was apprehended and changed by the grace of God, his entire early history was full of deceit. His very name is a suggestion of the deceit that was embedded in his history. Like Jacob's deceitfulness with Esau (Gen. 27:1-41) and others, the sin in the human heart will deceive the person in whom it dwells.

Sin deceives men with regard to its own *reality*, its own *quality*, its own *penalty*, and its own *continuity* (that is, it makes you think that you can stop sinning any time you wish, *or* it goes to the other extreme and makes you think that the situation is hopeless, and you will *never* be able to overcome sin).

Fyodor Dostoyevsky, the great Russian novelist whose writings penetrate to the psychological depths of the human personality, said, "Man is not like a mathematical equation; he is a mysterious and puzzling being, and his nature is extreme and contradictory throughout." The human heart is deep and mysterious, like one of Ezekiel's visions, which presents so many chambers of imagery, one within another, and it requires time to get an accurate awareness of it, and we may be content that we will never know it completely.

I was raised in the mountains of northwest Arkansas, where there are caves everywhere underground. But how deep they are, and how numerous, will be hidden from all surface observers. So is the individual human heart. Each sin is a part of a deep subterranean network, and it may be so deep and invisible that it is easily forgotten. It may even be overlaid with a multitude of other sins. James Kennedy said, "The average person has forgotten probably ninety-five percent or more of all the sins he has ever committed — but God has not forgotten a single one." C. S. Lewis wrote, "Man seems to think that time erases sin, but it is not so." "God requires that which is past," the Bible says (Ecclesiastes 3:15). Deeds are done, and we think that when they are done, they are done *with* — thus does sin deceive us.

Both the human conscience within and the recording angel of God above could join to echo the testimony of Pontius Pilate, *"What I have written, I have written."* The record of sin in human experience stands in bold-faced print both in the human conscience and in heaven. An old southern Negro spiritual says, "He sees all we do, He hears all we say, *My God's a-writin' all the time."* If we go on, heedless of our ways, unrepentant of our sins, unbelieving toward Jesus Christ, the time is coming when we shall be horrified and distressed as we reread the record of our sins at the Judgment Bar of God. The situation is so serious that it may seem beyond hope.

## II. The Removal of Sin and Its Record from Human Experience

But we discover from Scripture that there is great hope. We are now told about the *removal of sin* and its record from human experience.

The text from Colossians is one of the most dramatic statements in the Bible of what was accomplished for us by Jesus Christ on the cross. God alone can erase the dreadful "handwriting of my sins" and look on me in mercy, as I look on Christ by faith.

God has "blotted out the handwriting of ordinances that was against us, which was contrary to us, and took it out of the way, nailing it to His cross" (Col. 2:14). Here, the record of sin is seen as a ledger of *debt*. It is called "the handwriting of ordinances." The New American Standard Version refers to it as "the certificate of debt," and the Williams translation calls it "the note that stood against us," while the New International Version calls it "the written code, with its regulations, that was against us and that stood opposed to us." The centerpiece of this passage is that term, "written code" or "certificate of debt." The word Paul uses for this "written code" is *cheirographon*, which was "a hand-written document, specifically a certificate of indebtedness, a bond."

The letter of Philemon contains a great example of one such "written code," and it also carries with it the idea of indebtedness. In that letter, Paul states that his handwritten document is proof of his obligation to pay back outstanding debts: "If he (the runaway slave Onesimus) has done you any wrong or owes you anything, charge it to me. I, Paul, am writing this with my own hand. I will pay it back" (Philemon 18-19). In a similar way, we are under obligation to pay a spiritual debt. God bound us to a standard we haven't met. Our inability to meet that standard led to a staggering penalty, death. And this penalty is so just that if God did not impose it, He would be unjust!

The phrase "written code" pictures our sins as a charge list. It is as if a list of each person's sins has been compiled, and the person has signed it by his own history of sin. So it is the picture of an autographed promissory note or bond, and the fact that our signature is attached is evidence that we acknowledge its claim and our debt.

Our credit-crazy generation should be able to easily understand this. Most people have some measure of indebtedness hanging over their heads. Their financial mismanagement may turn that indebtedness into a Damocles sword which threatens to fall and destroy them. The bumper sticker which says, "I owe, I owe, so off to work I go," may be a nearly universal cry.

Here, the figure of debt is used to point out the liability we have incurred by our personal sins. In heaven's system of bookkeeping, your sins are debts recorded against you. This figure is often used throughout Scripture. Think of the similarity between a debt and a sin. A *debt* commits the *debtor* to the responsibility of *payment*, and a *sin* commits the *sinner* to the reality of *punishment*. A *single debt* gives the *creditor* power over his *debtor*, and a *single sin* gives *holiness, and law, and justice* (the sinner's "creditors") power over the *sinner*. And every slight deviation from righteousness, whether of character, thought, word or deed, only deepens the sinner's debt. Our sins are like overdue IOUs, each of which has, in effect, been signed by our own hand. Long ago, the Jews "signed" to obey the law of Moses (Deuteronomy 27 & 30). And the Gentiles (you and I) have "countersigned" through their consciences to keep the moral law as they understand it (Romans 2:14, 15). To combine the ideas of Jeremiah 17:1 and Colossians 2:14, the creditors are your conscience *within*, and the law of God, the holiness of God, and the justice of God *without*.

In a Dennis the Menace cartoon, Dennis was apparently apprehended by his mother while in a misdeed. In one picture, he is saying, "All I want is justice." In the next picture, he is sitting in a chair facing the corner of the room. In the last picture, he is saying pitifully, "Then how 'bout a little mercy?" Thank God that it is not necessary to face the justice which my sins deserve and demand. Since we are such sinners as we are, it is mercy that suits our case. Because we are such sinners as we are, we are bankrupt and cannot meet the obligations our sins produce. Sin strangles us, slowly, relentlessly, endlessly, like an unpayable, ever-mounting debt.

In recent years, I read the biography of Scotland's great author, Sir Walter Scott. Scott was a very remarkable man. His heavy work schedule in writing an incredible number of brilliant historical novels probably took him to an early grave. Midway in his career, a business firm in which he was financially involved failed, and his biographer tells us that "he had become personally responsible for unsuspected debts of 130,000 British pounds sterling (a large fortune in *any* day, and in *today's* standards, *still* a large fortune). When he received the news, Scott staggered to his feet. 'All is lost,' he cried. 'Am I left with nothing but this enormous debt?'" Dear friends, apart from Christ, sinful man is left with nothing but an enormous, unpayable debt! Walter Scott refused to plead bankruptcy, and began immediately to try to pay the huge debt. His health declined, and in time his mind and memory almost abandoned him. He thought he had fully paid the balance of indebtedness against him, but he "did not know that most of his lands remained mortgaged and the full debt not quite paid" (the quotes are from <u>Sir Walter Scott, Wizard of the North</u>, by Pearle Schultz). Just like many a sinner, who believes that his pitiful works will discharge the (enormous) debt incurred because of his sins. What an insane insult to the Law of God, the holiness of God, and the justice of God!

The text says that the note of indebtedness was "against us and contrary to us." The "note" is comprised of the law of God which each of us has broken. The text pictures a double jeopardy in our relationship to the law. First, it was "against us." It was against us because it contained obligations which we were responsible to meet, but could not do so. Like an unpaid bill turned over to a bill collector, the record of our sins was "against us." Then the law of God was "contrary to us" because it imposed a penalty on our failure to fulfill its obligations. Thus, the note became our enemy. "Payday always comes for a mortgage," an old adage declares, and this is true. Spiritually, the Bible says, "The soul that sins, it shall surely die." "The wages of sin is death." "Sin, when it is finished, brings forth death." This is not simply a dying into extinction, but a dying into an eternity of dying life and living death. This is very, very bad news, and it is true of *every human being* who refuses to allow Divine Mercy to rewrite his life.

Let me digress for more background to this dramatic and delightful text. Under Roman law, when a man violated the law and was found guilty by a court of law, a written charge was drawn up detailing the individual's offense or offenses. The written charge against the guilty party was often placed on the outside of the prisoner's cell so that anyone passing by could look at the prisoner and immediately know the offense for which he was imprisoned. In capital crimes, crucifixion was often the means by which the death sentence was executed. In the case of crucifixion, the written charge, or *epigraphon* (remember that word), was attached to the cross of the criminal. Crucifixion also took place along public thoroughfares so that all citizens could see the terrible price of committing a capital offense. In all four gospel accounts of the trial and crucifixion of Jesus we are told that Pilate, the *Roman* governor of Judea, had a written charge prepared and fastened to the cross. It read, "The King of the Jews" (Matt 27:37, Mark 15:26, Luke 23:38, John 19:19). Mark and Luke use the word *epigraphon* (remember that word!) to describe this document. John further informs us that it was written in three languages so that all passing by could clearly understand why Jesus was being crucified.

Our text in Colossians (2:14) speaks of the written charge or list that was against us. Paul uses the word *cheirographon* in the text. You can easily see the similarity between *cheirographon* and *epigraphon*. The first word is more of a *business* term, while the second is more of a *judicial* term. One might be used in a *bank*, the other in a *court of law*. *Cheirographon* is often translated as "a certificate of debt," while *epigraphon* refers to criminal charges.

The Holy Spirit uses the word *cheirographon* in Colossians to refer to the result of our sin. By our sins, each of us has created a spiritual certificate of debt owed to God. You might imagine this as a document listing every action, attitude, and intention of your heart that violates the law of God. It would be a comprehensive document including all sins, trespasses, and transgressions past, present, and future.

In the Roman world, when a debt had been repaid the certificate of debt was stamped with a single word. This was the Greek word *tetelestai*. It could best be translated "paid in full." Significantly, this is the very word Jesus used at the end of His death-agony on the cross. At the very moment He died, *an awfully important debt was paid in full!*

Now for the "bottom line." *Our cheirographon* — our certificate of debt — became *Christ's epigraphon* — *His criminal charges!* He assumed full responsibility for our sin-debt — and paid it in full! As He was dying, He cried out, *"Tetelestai"*, which means *"Finished! Paid in full!"*

The good News of the Colossians text is that a *Divine Surety* has taken up our case. Verse six of Colossians two identifies Him as *"Christ Jesus the Lord."* A Divinely appointed and Divinely qualified Person has taken up our case, and paid our debt! We owed a debt we could not pay, so He paid a debt He did not owe! We were bankrupt, but Jesus Christ became the Surety for an insolvent humanity! On an awful Day on an awful Cross, He measured out His royal blood in full payment of the indebtedness of our sins. As a result of His Death, *tetelestai* now appears emblazoned across your certificate of debt when you appropriate by personal faith Jesus Christ's atoning death on your behalf. When you and I say yes to Jesus, our certificate of debt is canceled. Our debt has been paid in full. We are forgiven. We must be very careful to understand the statement of the Colossians verses about this payment.

I saw a beautiful office picture that shows the interior of an old country store. In the foreground is an old-fashioned cash register. On the top of it, a brass "Amount Purchased" sign is over the window where *"Eternal Life"* has been rung up. The cash register drawer is open. On the wall beside the cash register is a bill marked "Paid", and a small metal cross is driven through it like a nail, pinning it to the wall. The caption at the bottom of the picture reads, *"Paid In Full."*

We are told that the Divine Surety made a *Decisive Settlement* of our sins on the cross. He "blotted out the handwriting of ordinances that was contrary to us." The word translated "blotted out" means to wipe away completely, a picture of total removal or obliteration. It is variously translated by our words, "cancel, wipe out, erase." The charge list of our sins, the composite tabulation, is totally removed from the record! Martin Luther daringly said that it is as if God "uncreated our sins!" The slate is clean, and we are completely exonerated! All of our incriminating failures are blotted out. No wonder Billy Zeoli said, *"God has a big eraser!"*

A little boy asked his mother, "Mama, where are our sins when God forgives them?" She prayed for an answer even as he spoke, and the answer came. "Son," she said, "do you remember when you wrote on the chalkboard in your playroom today?" "Yes," he answered. "Do you remember what you did to the pictures you had drawn when you were finished playing?" "Yes, I erased them," he answered. "And where were they when you erased them?" she asked. "They were nowhere," he replied. "Well, that is exactly where your sins are when God forgives them; they are nowhere," she said, and he was satisfied.

The text says, "He (God, according to verse 13) took it (the certificate of indebtedness) out of the way" (so that it could never again be found). Remember that it is the receiver of the satisfaction rather than the offerer of it who cancels the debt, so the actor here is God. The verb is a perfect tense in Greek (do you remember our earlier lesson in Greek grammar?), expressing the permanency of the removal. God through Jesus' death on the cross has totally and permanently removed the note of indebtedness and it no longer stands in the way between me and God!

We are clearly told where the note of our sin-debt was taken to and what was done with it. "He took it out of the way, nailing it to the cross." Jesus "took the IOU away." The original language is drastic. It means that God wrenched the charge list out of the people's clenched fists.

He took it completely away from us. It is not in our possession anymore; it belongs to Him now. The believer should have no fear whatsoever that the penalty for a broken law will later be required of him. Jesus has taken the record and destroyed it on the cross.

In fact, we could express the picture like this. When *man* looked on the cross, he saw the backs of Jesus' hands held directly against the wood of the cross by the piercing nails. But when God looked at the cross, He saw man's note of indebtedness because of sin suspended between the back of Jesus' hand and the wood of the cross, with the nail driven through it also — and it was covered and blotted out by the outpouring of His blood!

Martin Luther told of a dream in which he was visited at night by Satan, who brought to him a record of his own life, written with his own hand. The Accuser said to him, "Is this true, did you write it?" The poor terrified Luther had to confess that it was all true. Scroll after scroll was unrolled, and the same confession was forced each time. At length, Satan started to leave, having brought Luther down into abject misery. But suddenly the great Reformer spoke firmly to the Tempter: "It is true, every word of it, but you must write one thing more: 'The blood of Jesus Christ, God's Son, cleanses us from all sin!'"

Furthermore, God "nailed the charge-list of our sins to the cross." The actual nails that were used in crucifying Jesus are mentioned only twice in the New Testament (John 20:25 & Colossians 2:14). In the first statement (John 20:25), it is indicated that the nails went through the blessed hands of Jesus. In the second statement (our text, Col. 2:14), the nails went through the bond of the broken law of God. It is called a "bond" because it binds the Divine Standard upon our hearts. However, we have broken that Standard, and the law stood against us and was contrary to us. But when Jesus was crucified, the nails not only went through His hands, they went also right through the "law's invoice," that charge-list of our sins, drowning that list in the blood of Christ that flowed from His open wounds on the cross.

Repeat this to yourself over and over again, until it becomes "first nature" to you. The nails of the cross in piercing Christ pierced also the legal document which held us debtors and nullified it. The word that is used also carries the idea of nailing up the canceled document, in order to proclaim that a full payment has been made. "Paid in full," the document would read. "There is now no judgment against the debtor," the document would declare. What incredible news this is! This mighty thought has captured the imagination of hymn-writers and poets through the centuries of Christian history.

*"See Him ascending up Calvary's Hill,*
*Jesus our Kinsman-Redeemer!*
*Payment is made to the very last mite;*
*Signed is the contract and finished the fight;*
*'Settled' is writ o'er the hill in God's sight;*
*'Finished!' Oh, glorious Redeemer!"*

*"He gave me back the bond; it was a heavy debt;*
*And as He gave He smiled and said, 'You will not forget."*
*He gave me back the bond; the seal was torn away;*
*And as He gave He smiled and said, 'Think of Me alway.'*
*It is a bond no more, but it shall ever tell*
*All that I owed was fully paid by my Emmanuel."*

*"My sin — O, the bliss of this glorious thought,*
*My sin — not in part, but the whole Is nailed to the Cross,*
*And I bear it no more; Bless the Lord! Bless the Lord! O, my soul!"*

*"As a trembling sinner, I fear that God can never forget;*
*But one full payment cleared His memory of all my debt.*
*When nought beside could free me, or set my soul at large,*
*Your holy work, Lord Jesus, Secured a full discharge."*

Let me close this second point with a practical application and a vivid illustration. First, the application. Gather up in your mind all the personal failures you can think of and see them nailed to the cross. You should see every sin you have ever committed (or will commit) as nailed to the cross. Nail this down! Your sins were totally disposed of on the cross!

Now, the illustration, and I will admit that it is a somewhat daring, even controversial, illustration (it will likely prove to be controversial to those who *preach* grace but *practice* law). I will repeat it as it was told by a well-known author.

"The more common Greek word for the cancellation of a contract is *chiazein*, which means to write the Greek letter *chi*, which is the same shape as a capital X, right across the document. This was called a 'cross out.' However, in Colossians 2:13-14, Paul uses the Greek word *exaleiphein*, which literally means 'to wash over', as in whitewashing, or 'to wipe out.' The ink used in Paul's day was basically soot mixed with gum and diluted with water. It would last for a long time and retain its color, but a wet sponge passed over the surface of the papyrus could wash the paper as clean as it had been before the writing had been inscribed on it. This is the word Paul uses here. Our sins have not merely been canceled out; they have been blotted out.

"God made this truth tremendously clear to me when I was pastor of a church on the West Coast. I had been burdened for a pastor who had been defrocked by his denomination for immorality and had moved to my community to start life over as a watchman for a plywood mill. Over a period of many months, we lunched together and came to know each other quite well. I continuously sought to cause him to accept the forgiveness he used to preach and encouraged him to live as a forgiven man, but it was difficult for him, since he had lived most of his life in the concept that God has a separate standard for ministers. After more than a year, the reality of God's forgiveness began to dawn upon him. He and his wife attended our church, and he occasionally ministered for me. It was great to see this guilt-ridden brother begin to accept the fullness of God's glorious forgiveness. In time, his denomination recognized the change in him and reinstated him, offering him a small church to begin his ministry anew.

"The day he was to leave to accept this new charge, I phoned him on his job to assure him of my continued interest and prayers, only to be informed that he had changed his mind.

"'Why?' I inquired. 'I thought it was all settled.'

"'My brother,' he said, 'I just can't go through with it. After what I did in my last church, I don't deserve another chance. I'm not worthy to preach the Gospel of Christ anymore.'

"Shocked and disgusted, I hung up on him and went directly to the prayer room in the church.

"'Lord,' I prayed, 'have I been mistaken about him all along? Did he really confess his sin, or did he merely admit his guilt? Is he caught up in self-condemnation, or is he still guilty in your sight?'

"God's answer seemed to come immediately in my imagination. With my eyes still closed in prayer, I saw myself in a large room that had bookcases on all four walls with volumes of leather-bound books from floor to ceiling. It reminded me of a legal library. As I looked at the books, I saw that they were alphabetized by names of people. A large hand with an extended index finger began to move across the books, until it came to the one with this minister's name on it. The book was removed from the shelf, placed on a small table, and opened in such a way that I could see and read the pages. The first page told the story of his birth, and subsequent pages told of his early childhood, of his call into the ministry while he was still in his teens, of his first ministry and pastorate, of his courtship and marriage, and of his climb to a respected position in his denomination. I could only wish I possessed the ability to read as rapidly in real life as I was able to read in that vision. Everything that I read fit what I had come to know about this man.

"The top of each page was dated, very much like a diary, and as the pages got closer and closer to the first incidence of adultery, I wondered how God would have it recorded. But when the book opened to that date, *the page was absolutely blank,* as were succeeding pages for what would be chapters of space. Then when we came to the date of his repentance, it was fully recorded with a marginal gloss that this had produced great rejoicing in heaven. Following this, the pages recorded his progress back into faith, his ministry in our church, his re-acceptance into the denomination, and his call to the new church. Puzzled by the many blank pages, I asked if I could have a closer look at them. My request was granted, and I saw that there had been writing on the pages, but that it had been erased. n the bottom of each erased page, in red, were the initials 'JC.'

"True to His word, Jesus Christ had 'blotted out the charges against you, the list of His commandments which you had not obeyed' (Colossians 2:14, Living Bible). Heaven had no record of this man's sin. The only existing record was in his memory.

"Excited with this reminder, I rushed to the phone and called the brother. After I told him what God had shown me, he quit his job, took the church, and re-entered the ministry as a forgiven man.

"God does not forgive and then file it away for future reference; He forgives and then erases the record. The pages of transcript that record our sinning are erased clean. Even the tape recording of our confession is erased, so that none will ever have access to our past. The guilt is removed and so is the evidence. This is the way God forgives the repentant one. Acts 3:19 urges us, 'Repent ye therefore, and be converted, that your sins may be blotted out (Greek, *exaleiphein*).'"

The reality and the record of your sins were removed on the cross of Jesus Christ. So we have seen the deep record of our sins in our hearts and in heaven, and we have seen the Divine removal of the record, leaving our hearts like a clean sheet of paper. Now we are ready for the final point of this study.

## III. The Replacement of the Record of Sin

Sadly, most Christians think of the removal of sin and its record from the human heart as the climax and culmination of the Christian life. But forgiveness leaves the life sterile and blank if it is the end of everything in the Christian life. To be forgiven, to have our sin-list erased and forgotten, is a great gift. But are we now to be no more than a blank sheet of paper? Are we merely an erased record? Remember Jesus' parable of the house cleansed and empty -- only to be re-occupied with something worse than before (Matthew 12:43-45). Once the record of my life was full of *blots* and *blights* because of sin, but then they were cleansed away by the blood of Christ. Then is my life now only a *blank?* By no means. After the *removal* of the record of sin from the heart, a *replacement* is to take place. The *erasure from the page* is to be followed by a dynamic new *entrance upon the page.* A *rewriting* of my life begins. To watch God fill the empty space, writing a new thing upon the tablet of my life, is the greatest thing of all. That turns my life into the *blessing* it is intended to be. So Christ's redeeming work in each of us is two-fold: the *removal* of the record, and the *rewriting* of our lives. On the one hand, He says, "I will blot out as a thick cloud their transgressions"; on the other hand, "I will put My law into their minds and write it on their hearts."

Paul said, "Ye are manifestly declared to be the epistle of Christ ministered by us, written not with ink, but with the Spirit of the living God; not in tables of stone, but in fleshly tables of the heart" (II Cor. 3:3). In Paul's day, letters of recommendation were a common practice when persons were otherwise unknown. For example, in Acts 18:27, the Corinthian church received a letter of recommendation regarding Apollos. In Acts 15: 25-27, the church at Antioch received one from Jerusalem about Silas and a companion named Judas. Paul himself had written several such letters — one for Phoebe (Romans 16:1-2); one for Timothy (I Corinthians 16:10-11); and one for Barnabas (Colossians 4:10). Now he turns that common practice into an illustration of how Mercy rewrites individual lives and then uses the inscribed message to publicize the grace and glory of Jesus Christ.

A Christian is an autograph letter. Raymond Edman stated it well when he said, "My life is to be God's handwriting." Follow the analogy carefully. The *Author* or Writer of the letter is the Lord Himself. "Ye are *the epistle of Christ.*" The *"ink"* is the Holy Spirit. "Written not with ink, but *with the Spirit of the living God."* The *"pen"* in the Author's hand is the Christian teacher, preacher, witness, friend or disciple-maker who is used to press God's message upon the heart. "Ministered *by us,*" Paul said. Incidentally, this is a vivid description of the true work of a true disciple-maker. The *"stationery"* is the heart and life of the individual believer (hopefully, a disciple in the disciple-making process). "Not in tables of stone, but *in fleshly tables of the heart,*" the text says. Pause and think of how peculiar it is that Paul should use the metaphor of a letter, or a book, in connection with the Lord Jesus. As far as the Record tells us, Jesus never wrote a letter, or a poem, or a book. So far as we know, He literally wrote only once, and then He wrote in the sand. Why is this? Why should the Person who has inspired more books than any other person refuse a place among authors? Man can make a book, but only God can make and redeem a soul. Christians are in the world to be expositors of that which cannot be written into books.

I am a lover of great literature. I have a book in my library entitled The World's Greatest Literature. I have seen a book entitled The Book of Life. With all due respect, I must say that we Christians are God's "books of life"; *we are the world's greatest literature!* God says to us, "You are my Epistles; you are little living letters being delivered all over the world." And heaven itself will be a Library of such Living Letters, each written with a unique plot and message, and each should have a "Trailer of testimonials" of their influence in the lives of others.    My title for this message is borrowed from a Christian song entitled "Mercy Rewrote My Life." However, the verb tense should be changed. God is *continuously* rewriting my life, removing an error here, erasing a large stain there, correcting a word over there, erasing entire episodes along the way, and filling in the blank pages with His Story.

Do you know what a palimpsest is? You probably have used one in childhood, though you might not have been familiar with this big word. The word is derived from a Greek word which means "to scrape off." We are all familiar with a child's writing pad, written on white plastic, with the print showing through from beneath as we write on the surface. Then it is erased by lifting the plastic strip from the writing surface. This pad may be used — rewritten — again and again. So the Christian life is a Divinely written palimpsest. When we distort or confuse the message, God erases and begins again.

We cannot know too much about this idea. Look at the first three verses of the third chapter of Second Corinthians very closely. Here we learn several important things about ourselves as Living Letters. First, we learn that these letters are *unmistakably authored by Christ Himself.* "It is evident," Paul says, "that you are epistles of Christ." You can detect certain authors by their style. Occasionally, great authors have tried to remain unidentified in writing books or poems. There are many examples, such as Sir Walter Scott (when he wrote his early novels) and the Bronte sisters of Haworth, Yorkshire, England, who wrote under male pen names. But after a time, other great authors (Dickens, for example) began to guess that they were women, and in time their identity was known. We say, "That sounds like Shakespeare, or Milton, or Ruskin, or Stevenson, or Lewis." Dear Christian, the letter of your life should "sound like Jesus."

Consider the "epistle" named "Paul." Where did Paul get his height of revelation, his majestic contempt for the things of the world, his passion for seeing men reconciled unto God, the spiritual constraint that drove him tirelessly over the Roman world and provided the momentum for this one man to single-handedly (!) change the Roman Empire? Why, *Christ wrote him! That's where he "came from"!* Mercy rewrote his life! Someone beautifully said, "Paul proves Christ as a flower proves the sun." The great, indelible Divine inscription was carved into the parchment of his heart on the road to Damascus, where Paul got on the eternal highway. Paul did not start for Damascus and just stumble into glory. He started for Damascus a persecutor and murderer. When he "woke up" in Damascus, he had a new name, a new nature, and a new assignment. He was God's great Mail Carrier, and the epistle to be delivered was *himself, Christ-changed and Mercy-rewritten.* Jesus took hold of the palimpsest of his life and *erased a Pharisee* and *began to write an Apostle* in the same instant.

I could insert at this point the names of "a great multitude, which no man can number," people whose lives have been rewritten by the mercy of God — all of them unmistakably authored by Christ Himself. But let us keep our eye on the text of Scripture and learn something more about ourselves as the epistles of Christ.

We learn, secondly, that these living letters are to be *universally available to men.* "You are known and read of all men," the text says. These are not private letters, to be read for the private enjoyment of a friend and then stored in a box in a closet. They are available to anyone who has a love for the message they bring, and understands the language they speak. Ah, but this presents a problem, and reveals the solution these letters bring. What is the message they bring, and what is the language they speak? And what capacities must another human being have to listen to them and learn from them — and live by them?

James Denney, the great Scottish theologian, in his book entitled <u>The Christian Doctrine of Reconciliation,</u> speaks plainly to this matter. If you want to get maximum benefit from God's living letters, learn this from Professor Denney. "It is not historical scholarship that is needed for the understanding of Paul, and neither is it the insight of genius. *It is despair.* Paul did not preach for scholars, nor even for philosophers; he preached for *sinners.* He had no gospel except for men whose mouths were stopped, and who were standing condemned at the bar of God. They understood him, and such people find him easily intelligible still. When a man has the simplicity to say, with Doctor Chalmers, 'What would I do if God did not justify the ungodly?' he has the key to Paul's gospel of reconciliation in his hand." Dear friends, this is the primary reason God mightily convicts us of our sins before He saves us. You see, the tendency of our flesh is to always pick a standard that we measure up against favorably and use it to determine our moral standing. But God unsparingly reveals our deep-dyed corruption to our understanding, and His purpose in doing so is not to make us feel bad, but *to make us feel desperate—desperate for Him and His full salvation!*

If we are to meet God, we must lay aside our intellectual nibbling, our spiritual elitism, our elevated self-respect. These are fatal habits, attitudes that destroy the human soul. People who cultivate these things are blind guides who lead others steadily toward hell. They are too proud (and thus too stupid) to understand the forgiveness, the cleansing, the grace of God in Christ. If you will only realize that you desperately need to be saved, and that you cannot save yourself, God will move the universe to save you! Thank God for the despair that drives you to Christ! Heaven chooses to be totally helpless when we come in our pride, our cleverness, our efficiency; but heaven can rescue us miraculously out of these into God's sufficiency of grace which will make us sacrificial, triumphant, productive Christians — if we come in genuine honesty and humility. It would be much better to be in a dungeon of spiritual desperation than in a palace of self-righteousness or religious parade. When you have reached your personal midnight, God will shake the foundations of your prison and let you out — a perfectly persuaded evangelist of the Everlasting Goodness — and a living letter to be known and read of all men. The language of God's living letters is the language of a despair that has been met by a living hope, the language of a once-dead soul that has been brought to eternal life, the language of a slave set free.

Let me speak for a moment to those who "just do not understand," who "can't make sense of any of it." Friend, if the living letters of Christian lives are illegible to you, you are exposing the real condition of your heart. The full record of sin is still inscribed deeply there, and no removal has taken place! When Julius Caesar, the renowned emperor of Rome, was on his way back to Rome, he was approached by a messenger who declared that he had "an important letter" for him. The messenger urged him, "Please read it immediately! It contains an important message." Caesar tucked it in his belt unread, and went on to Rome — *where he was assassinated.* When they examined his dead body, the unopened letter was still tucked in his tunic. Dear lost friend, the committed, loving, Spirit-walking Christian is God's open letter to you. Read with care, lest the unopened letter be strewn on the pathway of your destruction. Any student of great literature knows that the cry of the world's greatest literature is, "Read me! Don't merely read about me, or write about me, or talk about me, but read me!" Augustine heard a child's voice in a garden, crying, "Take up and read! Take up and read!" This peculiar message from a peculiar messenger led the desperate sinner to eternal salvation. Dear lost friend, find a Spirit-filled, loving Christian, then "take up and read."

Christian brothers and sisters, we must remember that our lives as living letters are to be *universally* available. Jesus, who did not leave a written line behind Him, is now writing and publishing *worldwide*. The legibleness of Christ-written men and women is especially manifested in mission fields of the world. There, as nowhere else, it is the flesh-and-blood book that counts. The Chinese were unable to read the Christian Bible, but they could read Robert Morrison. What did the poor pagan American Indians know of the thirteenth chapter of First Corinthians? Nothing — until David Brainerd lived it out among them. Henry Martyn, Alexander Duff, James Calvert, John G. Paton, James Chalmers — what were they but living letters, known and read of all kinds and conditions of sin-darkened people without Christ? When Henry M. Stanley went into the wilds of Africa, he thought he went to find a lost Christian missionary. But *he actually went all that distance at such great expense — **to read a letter!*** Standing near the letter every day, he began to catch the Divine inflections, and finally succumbed to the message of love inscribed in the heart of David Livingstone.

People used to keep albums and ask their friends to write in them. On one occasion a young lady invited Robert Moffatt, the great missionary to Africa, to write in her album. This is what he wrote:

*"My album is a savage breast,*
*Where tempests brood and shadows rest*
*Without one ray of light.*
*To write the Name of Jesus there,*
*And see the savage bow in prayer,*
*This is my soul's delight."*

The first Christian documents were not manuscripts but men. The first Christian messages were written, not in parchments, but in persons. And the Mail-Carrier, the Holy Spirit, is seeking to deliver those messages to every human heart on earth. These letters are to be universally available.

Finally, these living letters are to be, ever and always, *unquestionably abounding with life.* "You are an epistle of Christ, written not with ink, but with the Spirit of the living God; not in tables of stone, but in tables that are hearts of flesh." Paul is certainly not discrediting the value of writing with ink. If it were not for documents written with pen and paper, we could not read these massive ideas which were transmitted through Paul's mind. He is simply admitting that life must not stop with print on a page, or writing on a parchment — it must be incarnated in human experience.

For your dead inner life to be made alive in Christ, then, is God's only way of bringing out all the fine, rich humanness within you. Recently, my wife handed me a letter and said, "Isn't that handwriting beautiful?" Friends, the most excellent penmanship, the most beautiful handwriting, waits yet to reach the page. Will you apply at heaven's throne room today, and ask God to so rewrite your life that the world may say, "I have never seen such handwriting as that! It is alive with . . . with . . . *with the very Life of God.* The more I read of it, the more I realize . . ., and the more I want what it is unconsciously publicizing."

Every time I purchase a book, I write my name inside the front cover, along with the date and place of purchase. Friend, you may have spent your life as the devil's copybook, scrawled all over with hideous and wicked writing that has sunk deep into the substance of your life. Your sins are graven on your character as on a rock. You may be like the wall of a public bathroom, indiscriminately scribbled with the lewdest obscenities. But God has paid an incredibly high purchase price to possess you. Would you open up your life to Him today like the proverbial "open book," surrender to Him, then let the new owner write His name inside the front cover? Then, as you walk with Him, He will begin to rewrite His message on the pages made clean of sin by His great work of grace in you.

While traveling from one European country to another, the famous artist, Gustave Dore, lost his passport. Without a passport, he was denied passage across the border. When he insisted that he was the artist Dore, the border patrol guards scoffed at him. Finally, one officer hit upon a solution. "If you are Dore," he said, "take this pencil and paper and sketch that group of peasants." Dore began to draw. In a short while, the sketch was completed. When the officers saw it, they were perfectly convinced that the traveler was indeed Dore, and not a deceiver. Every Christian is to be a traveler, crossing as many ethnic, cultural and national boundaries as possible to fulfill the Great Commission of Jesus. The Christian traveler carries two passports, one in his purse, the other in his person. The world around us will be convinced of the reality of the claims of Christ and of our claims as His followers when they see reproduced in our lives the features of Christ Himself. *Christian, be sure that the scratching behind the curtain is the pen of Christ writing out in you a living letter for the world to read.*

*Chapter 8*

# A MASTER FOR MAN

*"You call me Master and Lord, and you say well; for so I am."(John 13:13)*

According to the first chapter of the book of Genesis, man was created to rule. In Genesis 1:26, "God said, 'Let us make man in our image, after our likeness; and let them have dominion...over all the earth.'" So man was made to rule the world. Yet it is equally true that man was made to serve. In the very beginning he was placed in the garden to cultivate it and guard it for God, and as he did so, he was told that he himself would also reap benefits for his effort. Man was made responsible to God for every detail of his life.

Every man, consciously or unconsciously, is mastered by someone outside of himself. Some are under the tyranny of Satan; others are under the loving Lordship of Jesus Christ. But whether it be Satan or Christ, every man has a lord. He takes his orders from one of the two. Immediately we meet a difficulty. The slave of Satan scoffs at the idea that he is *anybody's* slave; he claims an unconditional "freedom" in his life. He is like the Jews who said to Jesus, "We were never in bondage to any man," conveniently forgetting their long national bondages to foreign nations in the past. While blinded by sin and Satan (II Corinthians 4:3-4), the lost man thinks of himself as "free". In reality, he is the pawn of personal selfishness and the slave of Satan. In contrast, a Christian happily admits his desire to be the "bondservant" of Jesus Christ. He readily testifies that Jesus Christ is Lord of his life, and only laments his own poor adjustment to His Lordship. In this chapter, it is my purpose and intention to assert that the only rightful lord for any man's life is Jesus Christ.

There was no theological textbook or statement of beliefs in the New Testament church. If the early Christians had a creed at all, it was stated in just two words, words that were like two sudden thrilling notes of a trumpet. The two words were *kurios Iasous*—translated "Jesus is Lord." The early Christians thought this to be the only creed that was necessary. It is the idea of the Lordship of Christ that I want to explore.

## I. The Fact of Christ's Lordship

Let's begin with the *fact* that Jesus is Lord. The fact that Jesus Christ is Lord is the central affirmation of the New Testament.

It is the first and most revolutionary fact that confronts any reader of the New Testament. William Butler Yeats once wrote, "Genius is the art of learning to live with the major issues of life." Whether men recognize it or not, the major issue of life is the issue of the supreme Lordship of Jesus Christ.

A few samplings from the pages of the New Testament should give sufficient evidence of Christ's Lordship. In II Corinthians 4:5, the Apostle Paul summed up the message of the Christian Gospel in these words: "We preach not ourselves, but Christ Jesus the Lord; and ourselves your servants for Jesus' sake." In Romans 14:9, we find these words: "To this end Christ both died, and rose, and revived, that He might be Lord both of the dead and the living." So the purpose behind the total redemptive work of Christ was that He might be Lord. Then, in Acts 16:31, in announcing the way of salvation, the Apostle Paul said, "Believe on the Lord Jesus Christ, and thou shalt be saved." Each of these verses, and many more, give evidence to the fact that the Lordship of Christ is the central affirmation, the cardinal truth, *the first fact,* of the New Testament. It is important to note that the word "Savior" occurs only twenty-four times in the New Testament, while one commentator who researched the occurrences said that the word "Lord" is found some 600 times. Slightly more than 150 of these occurrences of the word "Lord" refer to God, while more than 300 of them refer to Jesus Christ, and the word is used as a human term of respect several times. Look at just one book as an example—the book of Acts. The term "Lord" is used of Jesus 108 times, while the term "Jesus" is used only 67 times and the term "Christ" is used only 31 times. In the letters of Paul, Jesus is called "Lord" well over 200 times. Thus, I repeat, open the New Testament wherever you will, you are bound to see in its pages the evidence of the Lordship of Christ.

## II. The Foundation of Christ's Lordship

The first truth, the fact of Christ's Lordship, leads to a second truth: the fact of Christ's Lordship has a solid and infallible *foundation* under it.

The question may arise in our minds: What is the justification for ascribing to Jesus such absolute, unqualified supremacy? Or, to put it in other words: What right does He have to be Lord? What right does Jesus Christ have to claim your deepest love, loyalty, and obedience? Does He have any valid credentials? This question finds its simplest answer in the words of Peter in his sermon on the day of Pentecost. In Acts 2:36, we read, "Let all the house of Israel know assuredly, that God hath made that same Jesus, whom you have crucified, both Lord and Christ." In other words, Jesus is Lord by Divine appointment. He is Lord because God made Him Lord. But this is not an arbitrary arrangement. In the very nature of things it is fit and proper that Christ should be Lord.

One of the classic statements of the Lordship of Jesus is in the first chapter of Colossians. In that passage Paul grounded his claims for Christ on three tremendous truths about Him. Each of these is reason enough for Jesus to be Lord of your life and mine.

First, Paul declares that Jesus is Lord *because He is God.* In Colossians 1:19, we read that "it pleased the Father that in Christ should all fullness dwell." This "fullness" is the fullness of God. In Colossians 2:9, the Bible says, "In Christ dwells all the fullness of the Godhead bodily." If Christ were a mere man, then He would have no more right to be Lord than any other man. Jesus was "born King" (Matthew 2:2) and "born...Savior" (Luke 2:11). Supernaturally born, He is natural Savior and natural Sovereign. Like some majestic snow-capped Alpine peak towering high above all lesser peaks, nearer to heaven than to earth, Jesus towers above the plain of our common humanity: above us in His quality of manhood, in His sinlessness, in His inherent fullness of Divine life, in the Divine power that flowed through Him, in the authority of His thought and claims and deeds—solitary and incomparable—God in human flesh! He *is* man, but he is *more* than man—He is *God*, and thus He is Lord of all.

Second, Paul taught that Christ is Lord *because He is creator of all things*. In Colossians 1:16-17, we read, "By Him were all things created, that are in heaven, and that are in earth, visible and invisible, whether they be thrones, or dominions, or principalities, or powers; all things were created by Him, and for Him, and He is before all things, and by Him all things consist (hold together)." Four times in one sentence the phrase "all things" is repeated and traced to Christ as Creator and Lord. Paul groups together the whole universe of created beings and created things, and then high above it, he points to the majestic person of the unique Son of God. We find this same truth in the first chapter of the Gospel of John, the third verse: "All things were made by Him; and without Him was not anything made that was made." Jesus is the agent of God's creation, and thus He is Lord of all.

Third, Paul affirmed that Christ is Lord *because He is the redeemer of men*. In Colossians 1:19-20, the Bible says, "It pleased the Father....having made peace through the blood of His Cross, by Him to reconcile all things unto Himself." The New Testament bases the personal Lordship of Jesus over His followers upon this fact. His right to reign in our hearts is based on the fact that He died for our sins, and thus purchased us unto God as His redeemed possession.

The expression, "our sins", in the preceding sentence reveals why it was imperative that He die for each of us to give us the option of freedom from the slavery of selfishness and sin. Each of us is not only *undeserving* (we don't deserve Heaven) because of our sins, but we are also *ill-deserving* (we flat-out deserve Hell). You see, even the tiniest sin is a moral outrage to God, Who is infinite in perfection and holiness and "is of purer eyes than to look upon sin" (Habakkuk 1:13). He could have justly consigned us to Hell and forgotten us, but instead, He set His love upon His errant creatures and sent His Son to die as the Substitute for each of us. In His infinitely qualitative Death on the Cross, Jesus took the Hell we deserve in order to give us the Heaven He deserves. In I Corinthians 6:19-20, the Bible says, "... ye are not your own? For ye are bought with a price: therefore glorify God in your body, and in your spirit, which are God's." Thus, Christ has the absolute and unqualified right to rule as Lord because He is the only redeemer of men from the dire problem and the dread punishment of personal sin.

The great Christian hymn, "When I Survey the Wondrous Cross," closes with this stanza:

> *"Were the whole realm of nature mine, That were a present far too small,*
> *Love so amazing, so Divine, Demands my soul, my life, my all."*

## III. The Force of Christ's Lordship

There is a third truth which is absolutely crucial in exploring the Lordship of Christ: the third truth is that the fact of Christ's Lordship has a tremendous practical *force* for your life and mine. There is no doctrine in all the Word of God which has a greater practical bearing on life than does this doctrine of Christ's Lordship. It –He-- touches our lives at every point. Every decision that we make, every deed that we perform, every thought that occupies our minds, and every motive that impels us should be determined in light of the Lordship of Jesus Christ. Let me mention a few of the practical implications of this glorious truth.

First, if (since) Jesus is Lord, it follows as naturally and logically as day follows night that *we, and all we have, belong to Him*. This is ultimately true of every human being on earth, but it is *intimately and personally* true of every Christian. We must then live in full recognition and practical acknowledgment of the fact that we are not the final owners of anything, not even ourselves. We are simple stewards of all we have and all we are, and we are to be faithful managers of the total life-estate He has given us, and the result of our management is to be His highest glory.

Second, if *(since)* Jesus is Lord, it then follows that *we must obey Him*. When a person becomes a Christian, he voluntarily places himself under new management. From that moment on, his character, his conduct, and all of his contacts and relationships must be regulated by the Word of God. Today we have created an artificial distinction between trusting Christ as Savior and confessing Him as Lord. Salvation is regarded as a cafeteria line arrangement where we can take Jesus as Savior if we wish and pass up His Lordship over our lives. We can conveniently take what we want and leave the rest. Not so in the New Testament. You can't have a *"Come in, Savior"*, and *"Stay out, Lord"*, salvation. In the New Testament, to crown Jesus Christ as Lord is the same as trusting Him for salvation. The New Testament says, "Believe on the *Lord* Jesus Christ, and you shall be saved." The Saviorhood and Lordship of Christ are constantly intertwined in the Gospel mosaic and any attempt to divorce them emasculates both the Master and the message. To put it negatively, there is not one verse of Scripture about salvation that denies the Lordship of Christ or decisively declares that His Lordship is *not a part of real salvation.*

The Bible does not invite sinners to "accept Christ *as* Savior." Nor does it say "accept Christ as Savior *and* Lord." Rather, it invites us to believe in *Him*, to receive *Him*, and *it clearly tells us who He is.* In fact, the Bible does not tell us to accept or receive Jesus Christ *as* anything. Is this verbal hair-splitting? I don't think so. The problem with our slight grammatical change is that the word "as" limits. When we put in a limiting word, our addition becomes subtraction. The truth is that we should not qualify the Lord Jesus Christ with words that limit Him. We must identify Him Scripturally and then receive Him as the Scriptures have presented Him. Instead of dividing the Person of Christ into parts or offices, and choosing between them, we are to trust Him *as is.* We are to receive the total Christ into our total lives to meet our total need. When we trust Him, we surely don't know all that He *is,* and we may spend all eternity entering intellectually and experientially into that glorious knowledge, but we still receive *Him* when we trust Him to save us.

What kind of strange logic is it that declares that we can *trust* Christ without *obeying* Him? I must *obey* Him if I *trust* Him, or my trust will be mere hypocrisy. If you trust a doctor, you follow his prescription; if you trust a guide, you follow his directions; and if you trust Christ, you will obey Him. Jesus Himself said, "Why do you call me Lord, Lord, and do not the things that I say? (Luke 6:46). "Not every one who says to me,

Lord, Lord, shall enter into the kingdom of heaven, but he who does the will of my Father Who is in heaven." (Matthew 7:21).

A wise Christian philosopher, novelist and pastor, George MacDonald, said, "We must do the things we must, Before we do the things we may; we are unfit for any trust, Till we can and do obey."

Jesus Christ is called "Savior" 24 times in the New Testament and "Lord" many hundreds of times. Several of the 24 times, He is called "our Lord and Savior Jesus Christ." The New Testament tells us that, "being justified by faith, we have peace with God through our Lord Jesus Christ" (Romans 5:1). Then it tells us that we are to "grow in grace, and in the knowledge of our Lord and Savior Jesus Christ. To Him be glory both now and forever. Amen" (II Peter 3:18). It is obvious that we only do business with Him when we deal with the total person, and when we receive Him, it is that total Person that we must and do receive.

Adelaide Pollard wrote a great Christian hymn entitled, "Have Thine Own Way, Lord." The hymn closes with these words:

> *"Have Thine own way, Lord!*
> *Have Thine own way!*
> *Hold o'er my being absolute sway!*
> *Fill with Thy Spirit till all shall see*
> *Christ only, always, living in me?"*

It is at this very point that all the tension of the Christian life and all the tension in our society occurs between autonomous, self-centered human beings and the claims of Christ to absolute control of each human life. In the case of believers, a tense struggle between flesh and spirit prevails until the Biblical resolution is found (Galatians 5:16-17; note especially verse 16). In the case of unbelievers, the retort that "we will not have this Man reign over us," is the common and representative response, spoken or unspoken, to the claims of Christ. *In the church*, the tension is often covered in respectability by a celebration that usually stops short of His *full control* in every aspect of each person's life, and *the culture at large* is blatant in its rejection of Christ and His claims as Benevolent Lord.

Let the issue be clear. Before I can fully say, "*Thy* Kingdom *come*," I must say, "*My* kingdom *go*." If Christ's Lordship does not disrupt my own lordship (the meaning of sin: 'I am the Boss of my life'), then the reality of my conversion to Christ must be questioned. The prophet Isaiah, looking ahead to Christ's actual reign, said, "The government shall be upon His shoulders" (Isaiah 9:6), and "of the increase of His government and peace there shall be no end" (Isaiah 9:7). But today, at this moment, if I am to fully honor His Person and His Purpose in my life, the government of my life must be solidly and totally placed upon His shoulders, and there must be no reservations in my surrender. But this is not a mere stern and sterile arrangement. Jesus Himself promised specific compensation to us when we make this surrender. This is His promise: when Jesus becomes my Savior and my Sovereign, He also becomes my Sponsor! When He gets the keys to my kingdom treasures, I get the keys to His Kingdom treasures! This is not to be wrongly interpreted; this is better than mere material resources, though the promise may include that. The principle resources of the reign of Christ are "out of this world", but they are to be translated by each Christian into everyday living *in this world*! Read and re-read the book of Ephesians to be reminded of the inventory of these resources, or read and re-read I Corinthians 3:21-23.

I have flown to nations all over the world. When I board an airplane, I gladly give control to the pilots. I don't want to be in control, because I know that it is much better for them to control and guide the plane. They are infinitely better qualified, and therefore, it is best to give control over to them. I simply sit down in my assigned seat, buckle myself in place, and "abide" for the duration of the flight. By doing this, do I lose anything? No, I simply gain the benefit of their competence for my life. I could demand the "freedom" to fly the plane, but my insistent exercise of such "freedom" would only cause the flight to end in disaster. Christian, being in Christ, you can nestle in and "abide" in Him and under His Lordship. You can indeed "be careful for nothing"! He can handle your situation with His own skill, sense and supernatural ability, and you gain the benefit of His Omni-competence for your life!

Third, if *(since)* Jesus is Lord, we surely should *tell others about Him.* The idea of the Lordship of Christ is the very ground on which the Great Commission is based. "All authority is given unto Me in Heaven and on earth. As you are going therefore, turn people into disciples in all nations...." (Matthew 28:18-19). What an incredible privilege and blessing to be included in the greatest enterprise on earth, the task of "making all men see" (Ephesians 3:9). Since Jesus is Lord, we should never rest content so long as there is a single person anywhere in the world who has not heard of Him and had the opportunity to submit himself to His loving Lordship.

Fourth, if (since) Jesus is Lord, it follows logically that all believers ought to immediately submit themselves to Him. The Bible says, "If you shall confess with your mouth Jesus as Lord, and believe in your heart that God raised Him from the dead, you shall be saved" (Romans 10:9). If you are not a Christian, if you are unsaved, I do not ask you, "Will you confess Jesus as Lord?" for you must and will do that—now or later. Malcolm Muggeridge, the great British philosopher and writer, said, "We acknowledge a King that men did not crown and cannot dethrone," and I must add that He is King of even the person who militantly denounces and hates Him. The proper question is, "When will you confess Him as Lord—now, while both you and He can get the full benefits of that relationship, or beyond the grave when it will be too late for you to get in on the incredible benefits of His Lordship?" The Bible says that, one day, "at the name of Jesus, every knee shall bow, . . . and that every tongue confess that Jesus Christ is Lord, to the glory of God the Father" (Philippians 2:10-11). You will do it eventually, why not now?

It is essential at this point to mention what is perhaps the greatest problem in the Christianity we know. "Words are cheap," the old adage says, and it is true. It is very easy to give lip service to Jesus as Lord, but the test is in our actions. In fact, it is not mere action, but *obedient* action, that is the proof of His Lordship in our lives. We *speak* of Lordship, *sing* of Lordship, and *celebrate* Lordship in every worship service, but we may do all of this with no expectation or intention that our *profession* will lead to a moment-by-moment *practice that is totally controlled and monitored by His Lordship.* Somehow the coordination of these two things often does not "compute" in the lives of conventional, church-going "Christians." We profess that Jesus is the Leader and that we are His followers, but truthfully, we are often guilty of drifting into role confusion. I recently read this statement, "On a sinking ship, the passengers can do anything they like." But be warned. On the "Christian ship", when the "passengers" pay their fees and then merely sit down to enjoy the ride, they must realize that they are a very real part of the increasing lilt of the boat, and the boat will end up being an aimless derelict on the sea of life (or completely scuttled at the bottom of the sea) instead of the Lifeboat it was intended to be.

Paul Rees wrote, "The inadequacy of the typical evangelical message of His Lordship is glaring. We speak often of handing over all the keys of control to Jesus Christ, but to what real personal result? To what final product? Does it match the product of the New Testament? Of the book of Acts?" Christian, if all of the prayers you have prayed over the last thirty days were totally answered, what effect would this have on the global cause of Christ? I fear that honesty would drive us to a very sad answer. The word "Lord" is the supremely important word of the New Testament, and yet it is often the most thoughtlessly spoken word in the Christian vocabulary. It would appear that we Christians need to spend some lengthy and quality time re-thinking the Lordship of Jesus Christ.

A young student of Rugby boys' school in England approached Dr. Arnold, the headmaster of the school, holding a failed Math paper in his hand. Dr. Arnold examined the paper and said, "Son, you must think." The boy forlornly replied, "But, Sir, I did think." The Dr. replied firmly, "Then you must think again, and this time you must think correctly." Christians, it is certain that we must think again about Christ's absolute and authoritative Lordship, and this time, we must think correctly.

I have deliberately chosen to save this gigantic truth until the last pages of this chapter. In order to impress us with the absolute and unqualified nature of His Lordship, the New Testament occasionally uses an extremely radical word for Jesus as Lord. One of the Greek words for Lord is *despotes*, from which we derive our tyrannical word, "despot." This word is used in our common speech synonymously with the words "tyrant" and "dictator". This word is radical enough that it should serve to startle us into the recognition of the absoluteness of Christ's authority over everything and everybody. He is absolute and unqualified Ruler of all—and I don't get a vote about that fact. When He is really the Lord of my life, nothing else **can** be; but when He is not really the Lord of my seconds, and minutes, and hours, and days, and weeks, and months, and years, and decades, **anything** can be.

The Latin equivalent of the Greek word for Lord, *kurios*, is *dominus*, from which we derive the English words, "dominion" and "domination." The central idea is that of total control. The Lordship of Christ means that you personally submit yourself to His control over your entire life. Control is essential in life. This is proved every time we read in the newspapers or hear on the newscasts of some celebrity whose life is spinning destructively out of control, and we see this also in the common lives of people all around us. Without control, any factor or feature of our lives can become incredibly destructive. Gravity must control the planets, or they spin away into vagrant paths through space. The grace of His Lordship must control our lives, or they spin away onto a collision course with disaster. Control is necessary in life, and the proper control is advantageous. Neither you nor I can become what God designed us to be without the proper control of Jesus as Lord of our lives.

Speaking of Jesus, the Bible says, "You are worthy," and this calls for my total yielding to Him. It is only the unworthy in me that refuses to bow down to the One of Supreme Worth and Worthiness. In fact, when I face the One of Supreme Worth and Worthiness and do not respond by total surrender and submission, I simply expose the fact that what is unworthy controls me.

Dear friend, would you say with your heart today, "I, at this moment, yield and surrender myself to the Person of Jesus Christ and receive Him into My life. I want Him to be everything He is—inside of me.

I want Him to do everything He wants to do—in me and through me." At that moment, He will become your Savior, your Lord, your Friend, your Companion, your Guide, your Counselor . . . . indeed, He will become your very Life. You will forever regard this moment as the greatest moment of your eternity!

*Chapter 9*

# THE MAGNITUDE OF MAN

*"The word which came to Jeremiah from the Lord: Arise and go down to the potter's house, and there I will cause you to hear My words. Then I went down to the potter's house, and behold, he was working at the wheel. And the vessel that he was making of clay was spoiled in the hand of the potter; so he made it over, reworking it into another vessel, as it seemed good to the potter to make it. Then the word of the Lord came to me: O house of Israel, cannot I do with you as this potter? says the Lord. Behold, as the clay is in the potter's hand, so are you in My hand, O house of Israel." (Jeremiah 18:1-6)*

Even the best of men sometimes become discouraged. In our text we look in on one of God's great prophets, Jeremiah. God had called him to preach and to call Israel to repentance. He did the best he could, but it seemed that all his efforts were in vain. The people went on in their sins, forgetting God. Jeremiah became disgusted and wanted to quit. So God sent him down to the potter's house to teach him the lesson of patience and persistence. When he went into the potter's house, three objects at once caught and held his attention. First, there was a man at work, the potter. Second, there was that with which he worked, a bit of clay that was being fashioned into a vessel. And third, there was that upon which he worked, the wheel. All three of these objects have tremendous spiritual meaning. The *potter* represents God, infinite in wisdom, love, and skill. The *clay* represents man, pliable to God's touch, containing the potential of incredible development and usefulness, and whose life is in God's hand. And the *wheel* represents all the circumstances of life, the providence by which God seeks to make man and bring him to his best.

Dr. John Mackay, past president of Princeton theological seminary, said, "The crucial problem of our generation is the problem of man." One of the greatest needs in the world today is for man to understand himself. What can we say for sure about man? What is the spiritual history of man? The fourth verse of our text points out three facts in man's history about which we can be certain, and the New Testament revelation adds a significant fourth fact. This fourth fact is also suggested by the story of the potter's house. Here is a study of those four facts in the spiritual history of man.

## I. Formed by God

First, we know that man was *formed by God*. Man is referred to as "the vessel that he made of clay." As Jeremiah stood there to watch, the potter took a bit of clay and formed it rapidly into a vessel of beauty. Furthermore, the vessel, when completed, carried a design built into it at its creation. What a beautiful and perfect illustration of the creation of man! Genesis 1:27 says, "God created man in His own image, in the image of God He created him; male and female He created them." The Bible indicates that God chose to make only humans in His image. Also, it indicates that God loves human beings far more than He loves other living things He has created. Most parents take a great deal of delight and pleasure in the fact that their children bear their "own image." It means a great deal to normal human parents that there are other human beings on the planet who have their conspicuous personal stamp, and the parents hope it means something to their offspring, too, that they resemble the parents. The same is true with God and with those "made in His image."

In Genesis 2:7, the Bible says, "God formed man out of the dust of the ground." In Isaiah 64:8, the prophet pursued the same symbol when he said, "O Lord, we are the clay, and thou (art) our potter; and we are all the work of thy hand." Modern man often looks upon himself and his world as though he were not a creature but a god with absolute rights and authority. But the truth is in the one hundredth Psalm, the third verse: "It is He that hath made us, and not we ourselves." "He has made us—in His own image." No man will have true self-understanding until he sees and admits that he was made by God; he must see that he bears the "similitude" of the Almighty (James 3:9), but with serious modifications due to the intrusion of an alien person and the ingredients *he* threw into the human mix—and willing to explore all the implications of those truths. Is this truly important? Well, how you view yourself will significantly influence how you live your life.

Man was *made by a Person*. Man was *made for a purpose*. Man was *made* to be a *presentation*, a *portrait*, a *picture*, of God Himself. The Apostle Paul wrote that "man is *the image* and glory *of God*" (I Corinthians 11:7).

The word "glory" used with regard to both God and man suggests "the outshining of a radiance," or "the manifestation of a person's nature and character."

Exactly! Man is made to be *the manifestation of his Creator's nature and character.* The very purpose of our existence is to manifest the glory of God in this world. Just as a work of art is the artist's glory because it expresses the mind of the author and simultaneously calls attention to his skills, so it is with man. Simply by being what he was intended to be, he reveals the nature and character of God, and simultaneously brings praise and glory to Him. The question is, since man has fallen and been defaced in the fall, how do we live today like we were originally intended to live? We will deal with that later in this study.

Shakespeare presented the evident greatness of man, man made and stamped by God, when he wrote: "What a piece of work is man: How noble in reason, How infinite in faculty, In form and moving, How express and admirable, In action, How like an angel, in apprehension, how like a God."

Roland Hayes, the great African-American singer, had been born of slave parents. He was born in a tiny cabin in a former slave quarter of Georgia. His father died when he was only a boy, and he was brought up in poverty without much opportunity. But he had a Christian mother who raised him in a Christian home. One day, when a music teacher heard him sing, doors began to open for him all over the world. One of the highlights of his life came one day in London. He was invited to sing before the King in Buckingham Palace. He was overjoyed. He sent an excited cablegram home to his mother telling her about it. His mother sent a return cablegram. It had just four words in it, four words that only a mother would think of sending: *"Remember who you are."* Every man needs to remember who he is. You are a creature formed by God. This is the first fact in the spiritual history of man. Man was formed by God. However, we must brace ourselves when we say this, because the first fact is followed by some very sad, very bad news. One Christian philosopher said, "Though man's concept of the Absolute can never be uprooted, it can be seriously debased." We will now examine that debasing of man.

## II. Deformed by Guilt

We know, also, that man formed by God was *deformed by guilt.* Our text puts it in these pathetic words: "The vessel that he made of clay was marred in the hand of the potter." Man was made in God's image, but something has been superimposed over that image in an effort to destroy it. Man is like manufactured writing paper. The watermark of the paper is in its texture; that is, it is natural. The later writing on the paper is imposed; that is, it is not a part of its creation. In that sense, it is "unnatural." In his original creation, man's "watermark" was the image of God, and he showed natural innocence and purity. However, when Satan managed to seduce man into sin, that sin was imposed and unnatural, and it thoroughly defaced the original creation. Man retains evident signs of his original creation, but he is sadly deformed by sin.

Archie Bunker said to his son-in-law, "Meathead," "Don't you know that I am made in the image of God?" Meathead retorted, "Do you mean to tell me that God looks like you?" Archie replied philosophically, "Oh, I wouldn't go so far as to say that you can't tell us apart!" Even so, God's image is still in man, but it is badly marred.

In the simplest kind of symbolism, the profound truth of the "fall of man" into sin is pictured for us in our text. Man is pictured as clay that went to pieces in the potter's hand. Of course, there is a basic difference between us and the clay: the clay has no will of its own, no power of choice. Man does have a will and power of choice. The clay did not crumble because the potter has no ability or skill. It crumbled because of a deficiency that arose within it. Man can say Yes to God or he can say No to Him. You are called to cooperate with God in forming the finished vessel God desires. He has clothed you with moral freedom. You can follow His plan, or you can refuse to follow it. You can choose to obey Him, or choose to disobey Him. And the fact is men have said a unanimous "NO!" to God. *Man is a piece of broken pottery.* Look at the drunkard reeling down the street; look at the thief behind prison bars; look at the murderer on his way to the death chamber. It is *easy* to see that *they* have ruined God's plan for *their* lives. But so have you, and so have I. Your life, too, has been absolutely shattered by sin. Dr. Gilbert K. Chesterton was right when he said, "Whatever *else* man is, he is not what he was *meant* to be."

There is an old Welsh legend that says that Almighty God once held a great inspection of all the worlds of the far-flung universe. One by one the stars and planets and suns and moons passed by in review, and as each passed God smiled upon them. But when the earth passed, God blushed and frowned. Sin is the one great calamity in the universe. The vessel formed by God has been deformed by sin.

On every page, the Bible points out that man has been twisted, and perverted, and distorted by sin. As you thumb its pages, the Scriptural testimony mounts rapidly. Listen to David as he says, *"Behold, I was* shapen in iniquity, and in sin did my mother conceive me." Listen to Jeremiah as he says, "There is not one just man upon earth who does good and sins not." Or listen to Jeremiah, "The heart of man is deceitful above all things, and desperately wicked." Or hear Paul as he says, "There is no difference, for all have sinned, and come short of the glory of God." And John, the Apostle of love, declares, "If we say that we have no sin, we deceive ourselves, and the truth is not in us."

Ralph Waldo Emerson stabbed at this "mixed" truth—man made by God and marred by guilt—in these words: "Every man is a kind of divinity in disguise. A god playing a fool. It sometimes seems as if our world is an asylum full of insane angels. Occasionally they break into their native music, and utter at intervals the words that reveal their original creation—then the mad fit leaps out of them and they mope and wallow like dogs."

This fact must influence everything we do with regard to man. Someone said, "In one way, the most important fact in human experience is the fact of sin." Some years ago, a fellow Christian gave me a story that can be used to see the problem of sin. In Charleston, South Carolina, in 1983, a man was discovered by the police slumped over in his car which was resting at the base of a telephone pole. His car had apparently jumped the curb and hit the pole. Thinking that the man was drunk, the police officers wrote out a citation for drunkenness while he was still seated in the front seat of the car. Then, as they attempted to remove him from the car, they discovered that they had made a serious mistake. The man wasn't drunk at all; he had a fatal gunshot wound in his chest. The officers then surmised that someone had attempted to rob him and had shot him.

Here is the danger the Christian preacher, teacher or witness faces as we try to deal with lost people. The Christian community at large has often tried to arrest and reform what we think are mild cases of human misbehavior when in reality all men have been shot in the heart by an enemy who is bent on destroying man altogether. Each man lives with a gaping hole in his heart, and if not cured, that hole will prove to be eternally fatal. That hole is the present result of Satan's assault on Adam, at which time he shot a hole in man's heart that has drained the very Life of God out of him. Every mere mortal man born since Adam has had that same hole in his heart.

Furthermore, this must not be forgotten: the Original Artist is extremely upset with what the Enemy Artist, the Thief, has done to damage and destroy His Original Masterpiece. Also, He is upset with man, the vessel that chose to pour out its original Divine Content (the indwelling Presence of God Himself), refill itself with another presence, and engage in a conspiracy with that other presence to rebel against Him and "go independent" (the very meaning of sin). The attitude of the Original Artist will be seen in His reaction against the vessel that withholds itself from His restoring work. This vessel will be forever "a vessel of destruction," the recipient of "the wrath of God that is revealed from heaven against all ungodliness and unrighteousness of men" (Romans 1:18). Ungodliness and unrighteousness are the Enemy Artist's "ugly strokes on the vessel." God is an Artistic Perfectionist, and He will not tolerate anything that is not a reflection of His artistic perfection. If it were not for the Gospel of Jesus Christ, man would have absolutely no hope.

One further note about this deformed, broken vessel. Note that the text says that "the vessel was marred in the hand of the potter." Not "by the hand of the potter," but "in the hand of the potter." Any defect is in the clay, not in the hand of the Potter. Let me quote again from the genius of G. K. Chesterton: "In making the world, God set it free. He wrote not so much a poem as a play; a play He had planned as perfect, but which had necessarily been left to human actors and stage-managers, who have since made a great mess of it. We talk of wild animals, but man is the only wild animal. It is man that has broken out. All other animals are tame animals, following the rugged respectability of their tribe or type, the programming of the creator." Man is wild because he alone stands up to God, shakes his fist, and says, "I do what I want to do when I want to do it, and I demand to be left alone to pursue my own private purposes." That, dear friend, is an accurate definition of sin—private purposing—and the Original Designer must deal with it. And He has—and will!

It has been my privilege to visit St. Paul's Cathedral in London, England. I read the accounts of the attacks of the German Luftwaffe in World War II on London, and the account of the tremendous damage done to St. Paul's. One day, American newspapers carried pictures of the bombed-out ruins of the Cathedral. The newspaper caption read, "Designed by Sir Christopher Wren—Destroyed by Hitler." Even so, man was created by Almighty God, but he has been destroyed by Satan and sin, and only Jesus can recover him. From God's perspective, man is *sinful*, yet *significant* and *salvageable*. You, sir, may be *sadly lost*, but you are also *sublimely loved*. You are loved so much that the Great Physician wants to outfit you with a totally new heart.

This is the second truth we can be certain about. Man, who was formed by God, has been tragically deformed by the guilt of sin. Now, the marvelous third truth in man's spiritual history:

## III. Transformed by Grace

Thirdly, we know that man, formed by God and deformed by sin, can be *transformed by the grace of God.* The text says, "The vessel that he made of clay was marred in the hand of the potter; so he made it again another vessel, as seemed good to the potter to make it." This is hardly what we might have expected from the potter, but it is so typical of God. Jeremiah thought the potter would take another piece of clay and make that clay fulfill His plan, but instead he stooped and carefully gathered the broken clay with his hand, and placed it once more upon the wheel. What a symbol of the patience and love of God! When man rebelled against Him, God refused to forsake man. God did not *give* man up; rather, He *picked* him up and started all over again, remaking him into an altogether new vessel.

From the book of Hosea, there comes this cry from the lips of God: "How can I give you up, O Ephraim?" God does not throw us away. The marred life can be made over again! The life deformed by sin can be transformed by grace! We must note carefully that the potter did not merely patch up the old, marred vessel. He made an entirely new vessel. When God saves a human being, He does not merely patch up an old sinner. He gives an entirely new heart, an entirely new nature, an entirely new life! In II Corinthians 5:17, the Bible says, "If any man be in Christ, he is a new creation; old things are passed away; behold, all things have become new."

Several years ago, on a trip to the Bible lands, I visited the Vatican in Rome. I was intrigued, though saddened, by all the sights in and near the Vatican. Inside St Peter's, I stood before the statue created by Michelangelo named *The Pieta*, the sculpted images of Mary His mother holding the body of Jesus as it has been lowered from the cross in death. I looked at the statue with special interest because I had heard of the hammer-assault of the statue by a crazed Italian man named Laszlo Toth. Toth significantly damaged the magnificent sculpture by his assault before he was subdued by guards. Sometime later, the sculpture was restored by experts, whose goal was to repair the damage in such a way that no tourist would be able to see the traces of either the damage or the restoration. They accomplished their goal admirably; my untrained eye could not detect any sign of the damage or the repair. This is what God has in mind for each believer in Christ. The structure of man has been broken by Satan's assault and man's own stupid choice to agree with him. But the Master Repairman, the Original Creator, has moved in to remake man and finally deliver him from any sign of his brokenness.

Dr. Henry Van Dyke told the story of a portrait of the great Italian writer, Dante, which was painted upon the walls of the Bargello at Florence, Italy. For many years, it was supposed that this valuable picture had utterly perished. There were many reports of its grandeur, but no one living had ever seen it. Then one day, an artist appeared on the scene who had heard the reports, took them seriously, and determined to find the original. He went into the old palace where tradition said it was painted. The room in question was used at the time for storing lumber and straw. The walls were smudged with mixtures of whitewash and dirt. The ambitious artist had great heaps of rubbish carried away. Patiently and carefully he removed the whitewash and dirt from the walls. Lines and colors long hidden began to come to light. He knew he had found the painting. At last the grave, lofty, noble face of the great poet looked out upon the world again. Dr. Van Dyke closed his story with this application: "The work, great as it was, was not half so wonderful as the work Christ came to do in the heart of man, to restore the forgotten image of God." The question is, will man submit to the cleansing, transforming, restoring, revealing work of the Holy Spirit in him?

This transformation is not like that of a snake who crawls out of his old skin but remains a snake. It is more like the caterpillar when it dies and its crawling life ceases; but from its body comes the beautiful butterfly, a new creature with a new nature. "He made it another vessel, as it seemed good in his sight." Dr. Harry Emerson Fosdick once preached a sermon which he called, "No Man Needs to Stay the Way He Is." He was right! You can be a new person by the transforming grace of God. It was Sam Hadley, the converted Bowery drunk, who was approached on the streets of New York one day several years after his conversion by a man who said to him, "Aren't you the Sam Hadley I used to know down on the Bowery?" Hadley replied, "My name is Sam Hadley, all right, but I'm not the Sam Hadley you used to know down on the Bowery. By the grace of God, I'm a different Sam Hadley now." The marred vessel had been made over again! Billy Bray, the Cornish evangelist, used to say, "When I accepted Christ, everything looked new to me. I was a new man in a new world." The marred vessel had been made over again. And this same wonderful thing can happen to you!

However, we dare not leave this text without seeing the solemn note in it. Suppose the lump of clay had fallen to pieces in the potter's hand not just once, but a second time, then a *third*, and then a *fourth*. He might have patiently picked up the pieces and started again each time. But in the very nature of things, he could not go on endlessly. There is a limit even to the patience of God! This is the case because the clay becomes less and less pliable every time it is molded. It soon becomes so hard that even the skilled fingers of the potter can no longer mold it into shape. If you step outside the potter's *house*, you will find yourself in the potter's *field*. Right outside the house, you would find a pile of discarded ceramic clay that was shattered, or cracked, or broken. If you stepped into that field, you would hear at once the crunching of broken pottery under your feet. These broken pieces of clay are the fragments of vessels that might have been, if the clay had not resisted the potter. When a man continues to rebel against God, sooner or later the clay will be thrown on the scrap heap. You may remember that when Judas betrayed Jesus, and later threw the money at the rulers' feet, they used that money to purchase a potter's field. That field covered with the scraps of broken vessels would remind every onlooker of Judas — a vessel marred in the making, and then stubbornly refusing to let the grace of God do its (His) transforming work. The Bible says in Hebrews 3:7, "Today, when you hear God's voice, harden not your heart." To harden your heart means to gamble with the possibility of hell. To trust Christ means to be transformed by the grace of God. Which will it be for *you* today?

## IV. Conformed in Glory

There is one final glorious truth to be considered as we investigate the spiritual history of man. Man, formed by God, deformed by sin, transformed by grace, will one day be fully *conformed in glory* to God's highest plan. Every genuine piece of valuable pottery began as an idea in the mind of a designer. Just as an architect has a blueprint in mind before a building is erected, or a bridge builder has a plan for the bridge in his mind before the task begins of stretching the span across the river, or a seamstress has conceived the pattern of a dress before the scissors or thread are used to create it, the potter has a design in mind before he sets to work to shape the clay. The unskilled worker may create his design as he works, but a *skilled craftsman* designs first, and then constructs according to plan. He has in his mind a picture of the finished product, and that picture forms his model, his blueprint, for the work he performs in creating the vessel. God has a plan in creating the world, and He has a plan in *re*-creating your life in Christ Jesus.

You could call this his *predetermined* plan, and every potter has such a plan. If you could speak with the potter as he prepares to produce a vessel and you asked him what he had in mind, can you possibly suppose that he would say, "Don't be silly? Do you think that with all the vessels I make I have a plan for each one? Well, think again. I simply take a piece of clay, put it on the wheel, begin to shape it, and trust to chance or luck. If it becomes a vessel of beauty and usefulness, then well and good. I got more than I planned for. But if it becomes an ugly, useless monstrosity, that is all right, too. I simply toss it aside. I have plenty of material and all the time in the world, so I always work haphazardly and am never bound to a fixed and rigid plan." No, no, no. I have observed several actual potters at work, both in public demonstration and in their personal workshops. Never has a potter impressed me that he is devoid of design when he sets out to create a vessel.

Instead, the same potter I interviewed above might actually answer my question like this: "Oh, I know that it's just a lump of clay now; it's just a mass of ugliness at this moment, but stay and watch for awhile. It won't always look so plain and purposeless. Why, there is one place where that mass has already become a work of art. That place is in my mind. I have already seen a carefully crafted vessel in this apparently shapeless mass. In effect, I have dreamed a dream for this piece of clay, and everything I am going to do to it has the purpose of finalizing that dream, of emerging that 'carefully crafted vessel' from this hopeless and helpless lump of wet dirt. In spite of its earthiness and ugliness, you can believe me when I tell you that it is on its way to becoming *an ornament of beauty* and/or *an instrument of usefulness*."

Remember, dear friend, that it was *God* who sent Jeremiah to the potter's house! And it was God who intended His prophet to see His work in the potter's activity. It was God who intends us to read this account and understand the meaning of the potter, the potter's house, the wheel, the clay, the vessel, the making, marring and mending of the vessel—and the beautiful finished product of his work. If this human potter who works with clay works according to a plan, we can expect no less of God. Just as this potter plans every vessel he makes, so God, the Divine Potter, plans every human life. With *a plan in His head*, He works through *the pace of His wheel* and *the pressure of His hand*, and He will not abandon *the passion of His heart* for His child, whom He described as "His workmanship" in the glorious second chapter of Ephesians. While in Brazil several years ago, I researched Ephesians two in a Portuguese Bible, and though I am citing from memory and may not remember the exact spelling of the Portuguese words, I found that "His workmanship" was quoted there as *sua feitura*, which means "*His feature attraction.*" Verse seven of Ephesians two says that God is going to feature us "in the ages to come," that He is never going to get tired of doing it, and that we will forever be revealed as "His feature attraction"!

Note that the plan by which the potter operates is in His head. Sometimes we want to see His pattern in advance, but He holds it privately in His head. And He alone can transfer the plan in his head to the clay. The clay is necessarily ignorant of the thought in the potter's mind, but if the clay were intelligent, it could find that thought and realize it and manifest it by quiet submission to the touch of the potter's hand. Oh, the final result of God's plan for each of us is clearly detailed in His Word, and the general procedure by which He will complete that result in our lives, but the daily details are the combination of the wheel, the clay, and His hand working according to the hidden plan in His head. The God of the universe is working according to plan in your life, and He doesn't miss a stroke—or misuse it.

But God doesn't only have a *predetermined* plan for your life, and a *present* plan which He is working out touch-by-touch, pressure-by-pressure. He also has a *prospective* plan for your life, a plan for the endless ages of eternity.

In the creation, the design passes from the theoretical, the hypothetical, the mental, the ideal, into the real, the actual, *the intended vessel, the finished product.* The design that was held by the potter in his mind must pass through a formation process, a construction process, before the finished piece of pottery emerges. But finally, that finished product will emerge, a perfect vessel, "set apart, and forever worthy of the Master's use."

One day a pupil asked the renowned artist, Rembrandt, "At what point is a painting complete?" The great Dutch artist answered, "A painting is finished only when it expresses the intent of the artist." In the same manner, God's great work of salvation in us will be finished when we express in ourselves, and project from ourselves (like a finished piece of pottery), the intent of the Master Artist. Note in the text that the mended vessel was made "as seemed good to the potter," not "as seemed good to the clay." But what is the Divine Potter's intent?

God's original and ongoing intent is expressed in Romans 8:28-29, which says, "And we know that all things work together for good to them that love God, to them who are the called according to His purpose. For whom He did foreknow, He also did predestinate to be conformed to the image of His Son." Every Christian is familiar with Romans 8:28, but many do not know that the "good" toward which God is working everything in a believer's life is the Supreme Good of being eternally like Christ. It is God's plan that the Christian has only one Model, the Lord Jesus Christ, and he will finally manifest exact likeness to that Model. "You are a chosen generation, a royal priesthood, an holy nation, a peculiar people, that you should show forth the excellencies of Him who has called you out of darkness into His marvelous light" (I Peter 2:9). Both the Potter and the clay gain something in the formation process. The clay gains the means by which it can leave its uselessness and ugliness and become "something beautiful, something good," and the Potter gains from the clay the medium through which He can express His Ultimate Thought (His logos, His Logic—Jesus!).

A child's fantasy story will give us our closing illustration. "Once upon a time grandparents were in a little gift shop looking for something to give their granddaughter on her birthday. Suddenly, the grandmother saw a precious teacup which was emblazoned with the bright image of a human face. 'Look at this lovely teacup, Harry. Just the thing!' Granddad picked it up, looked at it and said, 'You're right. It's one of the nicest teacups I've ever seen. And the picture gives it great personal character. We must get it.' At this point the teacup startled the grandparents by saying, 'Well, thank you for the compliment, but, you know, I wasn't always so beautiful.' The grandparents, still surprised, said, 'What do you mean you weren't always so beautiful?' 'It's true,' said the teacup. 'Once I was just an ugly, soggy lump of clay. But one day a man with dirty and wet hands threw me on a wheel and started turning me around and around till I got so dizzy that I cried, 'Stop! Stop!' but the man with the wet hands said, 'Not yet.' Then he started to poke me and punch me until I hurt all over. 'Stop! Stop!' I cried, but he said, 'Not yet.' Finally he did stop but then he did something worse. He put me in a furnace and I got hotter and hotter until I couldn't stand it any longer and I cried, 'Stop! Stop!' but the man said, 'Not yet.' And finally, when I thought I was going to get burned up, the man took me out of the furnace.

"Then, some lady began to paint me and the fumes were so bad that they made me sick to my stomach and I cried, 'Stop! Stop!' but the lady said, 'Not yet." Finally she did stop and gave me back to the man again and he put me back in that awful furnace. I cried out, 'Stop it! Stop it!' but he only said, 'Not yet.' Finally he took me out and let me cool. And when I was cool a very pretty lady put me on a shelf in the main room of her house, right next to the mirror. I looked into the mirror, and was I amazed! I could not believe what I saw. I was no longer ugly, soggy, and dirty. I was firm, clean and beautiful. And the picture on me was the clear image of the lady who wanted me with her in her house from now on. And I cried for joy."

*Chapter 10*

# A MOTTO FOR MAN-CHRISTIANITY CONDENSED

*"For to me to live is Christ, and to die is gain."* **(Philippians 1:21)**

In twelve brief words, the Apostle Paul has summarized the Christian view of life and death. I have used two different titles for this verse. One is "A Motto For Man," the other is "Christianity Condensed." The verse is a compound sentence constructed by the combining of two smaller sentences. All the words in the sentence are monosyllables, or one-syllable words. You do not need to know the complicated language of theological jargon to live the life that wins. Here it is in twelve brief, one-syllable words. And nine of the twelve words have three letters or less! This means that this verse is the very apex of simplicity. Nothing could be simpler, yet nothing is more profound.

The two shorter sentences are separated by a comma. The sentence before the comma gives the Christian view of *life*, while the sentence after the comma gives the Christian view of *death*. There are three strong words in the verse, the words "me," "live," and "Christ." The middle term, "live," is defined in the union of the two other words, "me" and "Christ." When the two terms, "me" and "Christ" are brought into right relationship, I become "alive unto God." The human finds real life in union with the Divine. This is the only combination that truly deserves to be called "life." The word "life" stands defined in the equation of this verse.

However, in our foolish attempts to find life, we take other extremes and combine them, and we call the result "life." We sometimes say, "To me to live is money." Or, "to me to live is pleasure." Or, "to me to live is fame." But the New Testament answers each of these combinations with this verdict, "Thou hast a *name* that thou livest, and art *dead*." All other combinations fail. The equation is not accurate without the Biblical components. Life is the unique product of a unique union. Jesus said, "This is life eternal, that they may know Thee the only true God, and Jesus Christ Whom Thou hast sent" (John 17:3). This is the theological statement; our text is the practical statement. The word "know" in Jesus' statement is a present tense continuous verb, and may be translated, "go on knowing," or "be knowing." So eternal life is an ongoing relationship or union with God through Jesus Christ. Also, this verb "know" is the same word that is used in the old Septuagint or Greek version of the Old Testament for sexual intimacy. Thus, the Bible says that "Adam knew Eve his wife, and she conceived, and brought forth a son." So life is found in intimate, loving interaction between a human being and God. Paul's words echo the Biblical formula for life. "For to me to live is Christ, and to die is gain." Here is the simple secret of the Christian life — and yet, so profound!

## I. The Christian Life is Deeply Personal

First, the verse indicates that the Christian life is *deeply personal*. "*To me* to live is Christ." The words, "to me," stand in the emphatic position in the sentence. It is obvious that Paul is making a statement of deep personal feelings and preferences here. Jesus Christ is only possessed personally in the life of a human being. If these words do not comprise my personal testimony, then I am not a Christian. Martin Luther said, "Every man must do his own believing, just as every man must do his own dying." And he added, "The most important words in the Bible are the personal possessive pronouns, my and mine."

The Bible says, "God so loved the world" (John 3:16). It says, "Christ loved the church" (Ephesians 5:25). But this would bring me no benefit if I could not say with Paul; "Christ loved me, and gave Himself for me" (Galatians 2:20). The Bible says that Jesus is the "Good Shepherd who gives His life for His sheep" (John 10:11). It says that He is the "Great Shepherd" (Hebrews 13:20). It says that He is the "Chief Shepherd" (I Peter 5:4). But this would bring me no benefit if I could not say with David, "The Lord is my shepherd" (Psalm 23:1).

A cartoon by syndicated cartoonist George Clark showed two women talking over a cup of coffee. One says, "I'm pleased as punch with my weight-watchers club. Last week, we collectively lost 143 pounds among us!" But then she added, "However, I'm sad to admit that none of it was mine personally!" So where was the accomplishment? Where was the victory? She was not a real part of the victory or the accomplishment.

You see, dear friend, it is not enough to be closely associated with Christian people, Christian places, or Christian activities. You must know Christ *personally*.

A girl named Edith went to church every Sunday, though nobody else in the family attended. One Sunday, her mother met her at the front door as Edith returned home from church. Edith was smiling broadly. Her mother asked her what she was smiling about. "Mama, the preacher preached from a verse of the Bible that had my name in it!" Edith announced. "Really, what was the verse?" her mother asked. "Luke 15:2, 'This man (Jesus) receiveth sinners, and Edith *with them*!'" she answered triumphantly. Dear friend, unless you have seen the proposition of salvation addressed personally to you, unless you have received Christ personally, unless you have been born of God personally — unless you have heard your name as personally called by God as Edith did, you have never been saved.

Ruth Graham, wife of evangelist Billy Graham, could not believe that she was included in God's life. She struggled and struggled, trying to believe. She finally went to see a pastor with her problem of unbelief. He opened a Bible to Isaiah chapter 53 and directed her attention to verse four, "He was wounded for our transgressions and bruised for our iniquities; the chastisement of our peace was laid upon Him, and by His stripes we are healed." The pastor said to Ruth Graham, "I want you to put your finger on that verse and read it out loud, inserting your own name in place of the word, "our." She did so, and suddenly, God turned the lights on in her inner spirit. "He (Jesus) was wounded for *Ruth's* transgressions." She saw the truth clearly, and entered into her inheritance in Christ. Have you seen yourself as the personal object of God's love and God's search? Do you realize that Jesus died for you as if you were the only sinner who ever lived, or the only sinner who ever needed to be died for? The Christian life is deeply personal.

## II. The Christian Life is Wonderfully Practical

Second, the text indicates that the Christian life is *wonderfully practical*. Look at the second pair of words, "to live." "To me *to live* is Christ." Note that this word, "*live*," is a verb and not the noun, "life." The verb is the action word of our language. The New Testament is a book about life and living. If I were to ask you, what is the main theme of the New Testament, what would your answer be? Consider this before you lock in an answer. The words "life" and "live" are used over 1,000 times in the New Testament! This alone makes a strong case that the main theme of the New Testament is life and living. Remember that there are three strong words in our text, "me," "live," and "Christ." And remember that the word "live" is the word that is defined by the union of the other two words. Now, living is a very practical thing (!). Someone said, "The problem of living is that it is *so daily*." Exactly! And this is the genius of Christianity. It offers a concept that covers every moment of every day. Jesus said, "I am with you always." "I will never leave you, nor forsake you." If we walk (a practical word) with Him, He will make our lives majestic. However, it must be honestly said that if we don't walk with Him, *He* will make our lives miserable. You see, He is serious in His desire for relationship with the people He made for such a relationship.

A little boy was taking an elementary science exam at school. One question was, "What is salt?" He could not remember the chemical formula, sodium chloride, so finally he wrote, "Salt is the stuff that spoils the potatoes when you leave it out!" Well, Jesus is the One who spoils life — when you leave Him out. There is no maliciousness in the arrangement when you learn that you must breathe to maintain physical life, and there is no maliciousness when you are told that you must have a relationship with God through Christ to have eternal life. No threat, just fact.

The word is *"live,"* not dream, or wish, or hope, or theorize. The Christian life is a continuing experience. Can you imagine anyone announcing, "I'm real tired right at this moment, so I'm going to stop living for two hours and get some rest, then I'll resume the living at the end of that time." No, when a person stops living, it tends to be permanent! I don't live off of moments of inspiration or spasms of faith. I don't just live for one hour and thirty minutes on Sundays, and then go dead for the rest of the time. I live every moment of every day and every moment of every night. Even so, Christ is my life every moment of every day and every moment of every night. He doesn't live in me in spells and spurts and spasms.

Many people could be called "hypodermic saints," or "epidemic saints." When they get a "fix," an inoculation, of Christianity in a supercharged atmosphere, they excitedly vow that they will live for Jesus. Their roots are planted in the excitement of the moment rather than in Christ. The "epidemic saint" catches the high-fevered contagion of a meeting or a crusade or an infectious preacher, but he fades away as quickly as he started. He is a chocolate soldier who stays firm in a cool and comfortable place, but melts when the sun gets hot in an exposed place.

A true relationship with Jesus Christ means that every part of my life is affected at all times; every relationship in my life is involved at all times; every moment of my life is to be changed and transformed. Whatever living means to me anywhere and all the time — working or lounging at home, driving a car or a bus, walking along a sidewalk, shopping in a grocery or a mall, reading the Bible or a novel or a newspaper, banging a typewriter or answering a telephone, standing behind a counter or in a line — whether I am tired or in full strength, sick or well, happy or disappointed, whether it is Monday morning or Saturday night, "to me to live is Christ." The Christian life is wonderfully practical.

## III. The Christian Life is Gloriously Possible

Third, the Christian Life is *gloriously possible*. One word in the verse makes it possible. That word is *"Christ."* Paul did not say, "To me to live is to confess Christ," or, "to me to live is to be like Christ," or, "to me to live is to live for Christ," or, "to me to live is to pray to Christ," or, "to me to live is to serve Christ." These formulas sound wonderful, and are easy replacements for the real thing. No activity, or function, or attribute of the life must be mistaken for the life itself. Jesus Himself is the Source, the Secret, the Substance, and the Solution of the Christian life. Someone said, "Many people are trying to live the Christian life when they don't have The Life to live." No accouterment or accompaniment of the life is the life itself.

Captain Reginald Wallis said, "The greatest day of my Christian life was the day I discovered I could not live it, and God did not intend me to. Then, and then alone, was I willing to invite the Lord Jesus to live His own life in me." Some people say, "The Christian life is out for me. I just can't live it." I've got good news for you. You are dead right; you can't live it! And furthermore, you were never expected to live it as far as God is concerned. Let me say it reverently but firmly. God isn't so stupid as to demand perfection and then expect a thoroughly imperfect person like you to live it!

An evangelist asked a woman, "Are you a Christian?" "Well, I'm trying to be," was the reply, a quite typical reply to such a question. The evangelist asked teasingly, "Ma'am, did you ever try to be an *elephant*?" The woman replied, "Certainly not! What does that mean"? "Well," replied the evangelist, "you have as much chance of becoming a Christian by trying as you would have of becoming an elephant by trying. It simply isn't possible." "Then what do I do?" asked the woman. "You move from *trying* to *trusting*, and even then, you don't trust your trust, you must *trust the right Object, the Person of Jesus Christ*." A short time later, after further explanation of the Gospel and the way to be saved, the woman trusted Christ. To depend on your own effort is to guarantee failure, but to defer by repentance and faith to Christ's exercise in you is to guarantee fulfillment and fruitfulness.

Pastor Stuart Briscoe was on a preaching mission on the Isle of Man. A lady came to him at the end of one of the services and said glumly, "Mr. Briscoe, I just don't know what is wrong with me...." Briscoe interrupted before she could go further and said, "Ma'am, are you a Christian? Do you know you are saved?" "Why, yes, she replied, but I just don't know what is wrong with me...." Briscoe interrupted again, and politely asked her, "Ma'am, tell me in the simplest terms what happened to you the day you were saved." She thought a moment and replied, "Well, Jesus came into me." He said, "Excuse me, would you repeat that?" "Jesus came into me," she answered. "Please say that again," he insisted. She said, "Jesus came into me." "Again," he said gently. "*Jesus came into me,*" she said, and God turned on His light in her heart. You see, the staggering and stupendous reality of having the eternal Son of God, the Lord of glory, the King of all kings, literally living in her had never become a vital reality to her, and thus the Christian life was an impossible proposition.

Every Christian has a decisive line of demarcation driven through his life. He has a B.C. (Before Christ) and an A. D. (Anno Domini, "in the year of our Lord") life. He has a *Then* and a *Now*. In the B. C., or Then, time, he had to say, "To me to live is (his own name goes here)." "To me to live is Herb." "To me to live is George, or Joe, of Polly, or Sue." Then, by a glorious new birth, he became a Christian. This means that the center of gravity within him shifted from himself to Christ. Do not misunderstand this. The Christian life is not a circle with only one center, Christ. This would violate and destroy your personality. No, the Christ life is an ellipse with two possible centers, you and Christ. Now, "He must increase, but you (the self-centered, fleshly, competitive self) must decrease." As the false usurper, the selfish you, decreases, the true you, the you that you were meant to be, the you that you were born again to become, emerges under the administration of Christ's life.

So life is Someone Else! Life is Christ. Shortly after Malcolm Muggeridge, the renowned English journalist, became a Christian, he delivered a sermon in Queen's Cross Church, Aberdeen, Scotland, on Sunday, May 26, 1968. In that sermon, Muggeridge made this confession: "I may, I suppose, regard myself, or pass for being, a relatively successful man. People occasionally stare at me in the streets — that's fame. I can fairly easily earn enough to qualify for admission to the higher slopes of the Inland Revenue — that's success. Furnished with money and a little fame even the elderly, if they care to, may partake of trendy diversions—

that's pleasure. It might happen once in a while that something I said or wrote was sufficiently heeded for me to persuade myself that it represented a serious impact on our time — that's fulfillment. Yet I say to you, and I beg you to believe, multiply these tiny triumphs by a million, add them all together, and they are nothing — less than nothing — a positive impediment — measured against one draught of that living water Christ offers to the spiritually thirsty — irrespective of who or what they are. What, I ask myself, does life hold, what is there in the works of time, in the past, now and to come, which could possibly be put in the balance against the refreshment of drinking that water?" *Life is Someone Else!*

In the early 1960s, the heroic Christian leader Martin Niemoller came to America on a speaking tour. Knowing of his experience under the Hitler regime in Germany and of his resistance to the Nazis, two reporters representing large city newspapers hurried to hear him, expecting a sensational discussion of those war years. Instead, Dr. Niemoller preached a warm, Christ-centered Gospel message and yet hardly mentioned his experiences in Nazi Germany. The two reporters left the church greatly disappointed. As they departed, one reporter was heard saying to the other, "Six years in a Nazi prison camp, and all he has to talk about is Jesus Christ!" *Life is Someone Else!*

When John Bunyan was saved, he wrote in his journal, "O, I thought, Christ! Christ! There was nothing but Christ that was now before my eyes! O Christ! O Christ! O Christ! My Lord and my Savior! O Christ! O Christ!" It is *Christ* who "is made unto us wisdom, and righteousness, and sanctification, and redemption" (I Corinthians 1:30). *Life is Someone Else!*

And life is *someone else*. Note the subtle change, the necessary addition that is made when a person truly knows Christ. There is not only a shift of the "center of gravity" within him from self to Christ, but there is also a shift from self to other people. "You are *my joy and my crown*," Paul wrote to the 1 Thessalonians (2:19-20). *You* are "*my joy and crown*," he wrote to the Philippians (4:1). This is the whole point of the Christian life. We become fulfilled and gratified and useful as the focus of our lives turns from ourselves to Christ and others. When the focus of our lives is on Christ, He actually serves us, and, in a reciprocal miracle, we serve Him. When the focus of our lives is on others, we serve them for Christ's sake. If we only relate to Christ without a resulting focus on others, the Christian life becomes self-centered and mystical, an exercise in personal piety alone. This exercise appears wonderful at first, but it is in reality merely another caricature of the real Christian life.

On the other hand, if we sympathetically seek to focus on others without the monitor of a live relationship with Christ, we become mere social contributors — and soon that deteriorates into mere friendship. If I focus on Christ and His Life, then my relationships with others are incredibly sanctified.

We must realize that Jesus does not impart life as something separate from Himself. He Himself is the life which He imparts. "The gift of God is eternal life through Jesus Christ our Lord" (Romans 6:23). When we get *Him*, we get "*It*." "He who has the Son has life, but he who has not the Son of God has not life" (I John 5:12). He said, "I am the way, the truth, and the life; no man comes unto the Father but by Me" (John 14:6). We use this verse almost exclusively for evangelistic purposes, but it has a far more profound meaning than merely to say that Jesus is the only way to God and to heaven. After all, He said *three* things in the verse, not just one.

Explore the phrases, and let me interpret for a moment. He said, "I am the way" — that we might be *saved*. He said, "I am the truth" — that we might be *sure* of it and *sensible* about it. And He said, "I am the life" — that we might be *satisfied* just with Him. One hundred percent of Christians have gotten into the way and been saved. But substantially less than one hundred percent of Christians are *sure* of their salvation and *sensible* about their relationship with Christ. So someone is tampering in our minds and hearts with the authority of Jesus, because the same Christ spoke both sentences. But if there is a large decrease of participation from the first sentence of the verse to the second part, just look at the third part.

"I am the life" — that we might be *satisfied* just with Jesus, that we might find our *sufficiency* only in Christ. How many Christians do you know who have impressed you that they are satisfied just with Jesus? This is a very difficult question to answer. The only way it could be practically tested would be to remove everything but Christ and see if the person is satisfied. When the Apostle Paul came to die, he said, "I have kept the faith." You see, the faith *was about all that he had left!* But because he had lived a Christ-centered life, he was satisfied and gratified. How many Christians do you know who appear to find their sufficiency in Christ? Do you think you know *even one*?

Now, think carefully of the implications of the fact that Life is Someone Else, that Life is Christ and Christ is Life. Paul's equation is that Life equals Christ, and Christ equals Life. This means that there is no true life from which Christ is absent. Remove Christ, and you have removed life. Insert Christ, and you have inserted life. This means also that for any

Christian to know and understand himself, He must get to know Christ — personally, intimately, accurately, and well. Dear Christian, if you are to have an adequate and accurate sense of identity, you must get to know Christ — because *He is your Life*!

Now, it is just this fact that makes the Christian life gloriously possible. Sadly, most Christians still think they must live the life for Christ instead of allowing Him to live His own life in union with their personalities.

A father came home from work. He saw his son sprawled on the front lawn. "Do you want to play?" the father asked. "Naw, Dad, I'm too tired!" "Why are you so tired, son?" "I've been riding a horse all over the neighborhood," the boy said, pointing to his broomstick horse that was lying beside him on the lawn. "Son," his Dad said, "riding a horse shouldn't make you that tired." "I know, Dad, but when you ride this kind of horse, you have to do your own galloping." A Christian has the winged horse of the universe, Jesus the Son of God, to carry him, but sadly, most Christians still do their own galloping!

In happy contrast, consider the ride on Aslan (the Christ figure in the story) which Lucy and Susan enjoyed after he had risen from the dead in C. S. Lewis' great story entitled <u>The Lion, the Witch, and the Wardrobe</u>. An incredible story of redemption from sin through death and resurrection, the story climaxes with the two girls commanded to get on Aslan's back and ride. "That ride was perhaps the most wonderful thing that happened to them in Narnia. And it was a ride on a mount that doesn't need to be guided and never grows tired. He rushes on and on, never missing his footing, never hesitating, threading his way with perfect skill ... "To get the full meaning, do yourself a favor and read the entire book.

Go back to your childhood for a little while, and *enjoy the ride.* The Christian life is gloriously possible because Jesus communicates His Life to you and wants to carry you all the way home.

Every person on earth lives at all times in one of two verses from Paul's letter to the Philippians. The first is our text in Philippians 1:21: "*To me to live is Christ.*" The other is one chapter away in Philippians 2:21: "For all seek their own, not the things which are Jesus Christ's."

> "*Only two philosophies occupy life's shelf,*
> *Either live for Christ, or you will live for self.*"

Those two philosophies of life, that of the Savior and that of Satan, confront us in these two verses. Everlasting life is life with Christ at its center, but the other philosophy, that of self-serving, created Satan and agrees with him — and the person who lives that way will have to endure Satan's company forever! Let's finally consider the permanent consequences of the Christ-centered life.

## IV. The Christian Life is Eternally Profitable

When a person says, "To me to live is Christ," he will enjoy Christ's company forever. The Christian life is *eternally profitable.* "To me to live is Christ, and *to die is gain.*" A Christian can live or he can die — but he cannot lose! The word translated "gain" in this verse is "*kerdos,*" which means gain in the sense of "profit." It was used often in the secular writing of Paul's day to refer to interest gained on invested money. In II Timothy 1:12, Paul spoke of his faith as a deposit (the KJV translates it "commit") of his whole life into Christ's keeping. According to Colossians 3:3 and other Scriptures, this means that Paul's whole destiny went into Heaven's triple-padlocked Safety Deposit Box. We often call this Eternal Security, and it is exactly that. But it is not a mere sterile idea; it is part of a dynamic relationship.

You see, the only person who can give Paul's analysis of *death* is the person who is living out Paul's analysis of *life*. Only the person who can truthfully say, "To me to live is Christ," can fully, accurately and faithfully say, "And to die is gain." If a person belongs to Christ in life, he will also belong to Christ in death, and there is victory either way. The Moffatt translation says, "Death means gain." If Christ is my life, then death must be "*gain*," because it simply means that I get much, much more of what I was living for — Christ! When the time came for Paul to die — he was beheaded near Rome, according to history — you might have said to him, "Do you see the Emperor's executioner approaching?" Paul might have answered, "No, but I see Christ!"

Death meant just one thing to Paul, and that was a complete and unhampered union with Jesus. Paul talked freely, naturally and realistically about death. He called it "the last enemy," because it is just that. Paul never denied its stark reality, nor did he evade its imminence. It is a sure sign of our carnal-mindedness, immaturity, and insecurity that we moderns do not talk of death except in hush-hush voice or in somber tone and tragic mood. Or we swing to the other extreme, the "Pollyanna" mood of denial, deliberately acting as if we are invincible or that we will face the dark "king of terrors" only when he gallops across our path. Meanwhile, "eat, drink, and be merry" is our mediocre lifestyle. But Paul not only talked freely and naturally about death; he actually looked forward eagerly to the experience. He knew that death was the limousine that would transport him into the King's Presence, and though the last few miles of the ride might be very rough and bumpy, that "it will be worth it all, when we see Jesus!"

It is the clear teaching of Scripture that *death has two sides to it*, and not just one. For example, Jesus spoke of death as "sleep," and sleep has wakefulness both before and *after* it. Death is an "exodus," and we cannot imagine an exodus from one place without an entrance into another. Death has a before and an after, and one Person holds the key to victory in the life *before* death and in the life *after* death. In the context of verse 21, our text uses a large and expansive word for death. In verse 23, it is referred to as a "departure." Paul said, "I have a desire to depart and be with Christ, which is far better." He pictures himself as occupying a "narrow place", like a man walking down a narrow corridor between two solid walls. Paul is between two "pulls," one outward toward his earthly companions, the other upward toward Heaven. He says, "My preference, my desire, is to depart and be with Christ." That is the "*gain*" of death to a Christian.

The word "depart" (verse 23) is another of those treasure-packed words of Scripture. In Paul's day, it was often used as a *soldier's* term, and it meant to take down a tent — to loosen and remove the pegs, to fold up the fabric, to break camp and to prepare to move to a new location. II Corinthians 5:1 says, "We (Christians) know, that if our earthly house of this tabernacle (portable tent) be dissolved (the work death does), we have a building of God, a house (a permanent residence, unlike a portable tent) not made with hands, eternal in the heavens."

Then the word "depart" is a *sailor's* term, and it meant to loosen the cables and set sail. Think of it. A ship is moored at dockside in a harbor. Then it loosens its moorings and moves out to the threat and the adventure and the prospect of the high seas. Friends and loved ones in the harbor might weep over the departing passengers and say, "Farewell." But a while later, in a distant harbor, other friends and relatives might smile as they hear the cry, "Ship ahoy!" and a few minutes later, the passengers will receive warm and wonderful welcomes from those who greet them in the new land. So is death to a Christian.

The word "depart" is also a *sojourner's* word, and it simply means to move from one location to another. You see, when a Christian dies, he *only changes location, he does not change companionship*. Who is going to heaven? Those who live in a vital relationship with Christ on earth; those who can validly say, "To me to live is Christ."

If we are to adequately explore the phrase, "and to die is gain," we must at least briefly inventory the Christian's "Death Benefits." In what sense is it true for a Christian to say, "To me ... to die is gain"?

Death is gain for a Christian, first, because it will mean eternal *freedom* from the *problems* of life. As incredible as it may seem, there is coming a time (an eternity!) for a Christian when he will never *sin* again, never *suffer* again, and never *struggle* again! "To die is gain."

Second, death is gain for a Christian because it will mean an eternal *future* in a *place*. Jesus said to His disciples, "I go to prepare a place for you." Note the words "prepare" and "place," and remind yourself that Jesus was a carpenter while here on earth. As of this writing, He has been in Heaven for about 2,000 years — and possibly He has done a considerable amount of *interior decorating* on the place — "for you"! If the language used to describe it in Revelation 21 and 22 is literal language, then it is unbelievably beautiful. If the language is figurative, then the place itself is even more beautiful than figurative language can describe.

Two Christian men died together and entered heaven together. As they were touring the premises, one exclaimed, "Man! This place is spectacular! Why didn't someone tell us in advance how beautiful it was?" The other excitedly replied, "And just think of it! We could have been here ten years sooner if we hadn't eaten all those health foods!" Forgive the facetiousness, but this is something to laugh about and to celebrate. When the prospect has materialized into reality, you may be sure that we will laugh and shout and sing and celebrate — and I am sure there will be enough fuel for our celebration to last forever!

Finally, death is gain for a Christian because it will mark the beginning of unhindered eternal *fellowship* with a *Person*. Jesus said, "I go to prepare a place for you, that where I am, there you may be also." In His great high priestly prayer in John 17, Jesus prayed, "Father, I will that they also, whom You have given to me, be with me where I am."

A dentist had an upstairs office. One day, he was working on a patient in the dental chair. Suddenly, they both heard a loud scratching sound at the door. The dentist laughed as he explained, "That's my dog. I left him downstairs. He has never been in this room; he doesn't even know that it would be a safe place. But he knows that I am here, and he just wants to be with me." It might greatly impress some people to be told that the streets of heaven are made of gold, the walls of jasper, and the gates of pearl. But when a person has lived by this standard, "To me to live is Christ," he would have only one criterion in evaluating heaven: "Forget the furniture of the place, and its location. I want to know one thing: *Is Jesus there?*"

> *"My knowledge of that place is small*
> *The eye of faith is dim;*
> *But it is enough that Christ knows all*
> *And I shall be with Him."*

I want to ask you, dear friend, to finish my sermon for me. The method will be simple. Dare to write out your life philosophy in an honest sentence. If someone were to ask you, "In a word, what are you living for?" what would you say? In a word, what is your dominant aim or motive in life? Perhaps you would have to reply, "To me to live is *money*." Or, "to me to live is *pleasure*." Or, "to me to live is *fame*." Or perhaps your philosophy would be the all-inclusive one, "To me to live is *self*." Now, dare to finish the sentence of Philippians 1:21: "And to die is ... " If you must admit that life to you is summarized in a quest for money, then to die is certainly not gain; it is rather loss, because you can't take it with you. Billy Sunday added, "And if you could, it would melt where you are going!" If life for you is summarized as a quest for pleasure, then to die is loss, because God will not cater to your selfish appetites, sensations, and thrills. Any other motive will end up holding the same loss!

The only person who can say, "To me ... to die is gain," is the person who has happily adopted this lifestyle, "To me to live is Christ." You see, dear friend, "Heaven holds all of that for which you sigh," but it is only yours if you can say, "To me to live is Christ." If Christ is your very life now, He will be your very life forever. "Do you not see that executioner, Paul?" "No, I see no executioner." "*Then what do you see?*" "*Ever and always, I see only Christ.*"

*Chapter 11*

# SO, WHAT IS MAN?

In answering the question that provided the title for this book, is there a summary answer? Is there a bottom line? "The whole definition of man"—what is it? Is there a line in the Manufacturer's Manual, or an abundance of definitive lines, that ends our quest in a concise way? It may seem strange, but the answer is a dogmatic, unequivocal, unarguable, infallible "Yes". Indeed, that *will* sound extremely strange in this age of *dogmatic* relativism, and syncretism, and inevitable confusion and increasing uncertainty.

The question was asked and recorded in the Bible centuries before Christ (Psalm 8), and the answer following the question indicated that man is somewhere between angel and ape, "a little lower than the angels" and "a little higher than the brutes." After all these centuries, in the thinking of psychology, philosophy, science and history, the jury is still out. The question remains unanswered in the thinking of most, though individuals and philosophies sometimes have dogmatic answers.

Our generation has widened the gap between two answers. One answer is fashioned by *pride* in man's intelligence, ingenuity, inventiveness and advances. His intelligence has pushed back the boundaries of the universe to intimidating distances. His ingenuity and inventiveness have conquered great vistas of distance, nature and disease. "Indomitable man is Victor at last," said one vain writer. Because of these advances, man-at-large has persuaded himself that he can easily break all moorings between himself and God and go it alone, playing his capability against all challenges. This is the answer fashioned by man's pride.

At the other extreme we find a weak, poignant answer fashioned by *pessimism*. This answer comes in a mix of self-pity, helplessness, anger, hostility, protest, frustration and a thousand other self-addicted cries against "the fates" for making poor, poor man the victim of an indifferent past, a more insecure present, and a predictably insane future. We know something is wrong with man, but we choose to allow the malady to remain nameless, because then we have to admit no blame and seek no forgiveness. The truth is that we are members of a guilty race, and as sinners, each of us has contributed to the bad moral stock of mankind — but man-at-large accepts and confesses no blame, so matters get worse and man's pessimism enlarges.

It is self-evident that neither of these answers satisfies the seeker, and neither gratifies the heart. Why? The Biblical answer, the Christian answer is that these answers cannot satisfy or gratify the thinking man because neither answer faces what man was made and meant to be. G. K. Chesterton pinpointed the dilemma when he wrote, "Whatever else man is, he is not what he was made or meant to be." So what was man made to be? What was the intent of the Maker regarding man?

The Bible decidedly discounts the answers of pride and pessimism, declaring that man cannot be understood if we see him either as a *victor* or a *victim*. Then Biblically, what was man made and meant to be? *God made man to be a **vehicle**, a channel, a conduit.* He is meant to be *a carrier and a conveyor of a Person and power far greater than he.* He is made to be a receptacle and a release-point for God's own Person. But, as a vehicle, he may default into carrying and conveying a wrong thing instead of the right Thing he was made to carry. Thus, the entire answer to man's nature, actions and destiny lies in what he permits himself to become the vehicle for.

One possibility is that he will be a carrier and conveyor of sin and Satan. This is true of every unredeemed, unregenerate human being, no matter what show of "goodness" or "decency" defines him. "The heart of the sons of men is full of evil" (Ecclesiastes 8:11). "What is in the well comes up in the bucket." "Garbage in, garbage out." So man's heart is like the ruptured oil well in the waters of the Gulf, spewing forth that which it contains, and contaminating everything it reaches. "The heart of man is deceitful above all things, and desperately wicked" (Jeremiah 17:9). Recall our study about the "Progression" of man, and note that I am speaking here about *fallen* man, man diseased, disfigured, devastated, and deadened by sin (the present natural condition of every human being, and the continuing condition of every unsaved man).

The other possibility is that man may be a carrier and conveyor, a *vehicle* of God and righteousness. He may be a conduit for the Person and work of the Holy Spirit of God, manifesting the Life and love of Christ wherever he goes. We will examine this possibility more closely in the study.

# I. The Meaning of Man as Seen in the Old Testament

First, we will look for *the meaning of man as it may be seen in the Old Testament.*

It is commanding to see how often this view of man, that of man as a vehicle, is presented in the Old Testament. It is nearly rhythmic in its beat, a staccato rhythm on the pages of the Old Testament.

Go all the way back to the matchless story that is presented on the Bible's very first pages and you will find the source of this entire idea of man. In Genesis one and two, God fashioned from dust, with His own hands, the form of man, much as a sculptor shapes his clay. The product is and remains the lifeless clay model of a man, until God breathes His own Divine Life into it, and man becomes "a living soul". It is not possible for thinking man to form a more noble, more glorious, conception of man than that. Man the clay creature is the recipient of the very Life of God!

Throughout the pages of the Old Testament, the prophets of God declare that "the Word of the Lord came" into and through them. Jeremiah said that it was a burning fire dammed up in his bones, and if he remained silent, the fire blazed and roared within him. These prophets ("one who speaks for God before others") offered nothing of their own thoughts and reflections. In fact, Peter said that they often did not even understand their own message—they were mere messengers, mere *vehicles* of the words of Another. They were spokesmen of God and His Word, and articulated God's thoughts into words.

The prophet Ezekiel was even more dramatic in defining his mission as God's vehicle. He said that "the hand of the Lord was upon me," and that God carried him where He wanted him to go, engineered him to do what He wanted him to do, and brought him to bear what hardships He wanted him to endure. Ezekiel was *willingly helpless in the hands of God—as His vehicle.* He was in God's tight grasp, the channel for His power.

Even more daring is the declaration in the Book of Isaiah about Cyrus, the pagan emperor of Persia: "I am the Lord, who made all things…who says of Cyrus, 'He is my shepherd, and he shall fulfill all of my purpose…' Thus says the Lord to his anointed, to Cyrus, whose right hand I have grasped, to subdue nations before him…For the sake of my servant, Jacob, and Israel my chosen, I call you by your name, I surname you, though you do not know me… I gird you, though you do not know me, that men may know, from the rising of the sun and from the west, that there is none besides me" (Isaiah 44:28ff). Here, the Ruler and Judge of all the earth, overwhelms rulers and nations to work out His sovereign will. Incredibly, Cyrus, a pagan king, whether ignorant of God's purpose or intelligent about it, is His vehicle. Here is a wicked emperor, strutting in pride among his conquered peoples, not knowing God's will, but who in all of his might and ignorance is only the agent of God's will, the servant of God's purpose, the vehicle of God's purpose!

I have been captivated again and again by this line in Proverbs 20:27, "The spirit of man is the candle (or lamp) of the Lord." I have used this sentence again and again to illustrate the nature of man. But for this message, this verse presents man as the bearer of an inward light, lit by God. Do not misunderstand this statement; man is not the natural bearer of a "divine spark" which is poised, waiting to be fanned into the full blaze of deity. No, this is God's own light installed within a man so that he serves as a vehicle of that light. When God kindles the candle, or lamp, man is a lantern in the hand of God. "In His light, we see light" (Psalm 36:9)—and that light is to be released into the world through His carriers, *His vehicles.* It is God's intention that the gloom of this world be penetrated, illuminated and relieved by the gleam of His light, shining brightly through His vehicles.

These are but samples of this consistent truth in the Old Testament, that man is the *vehicle of God's Life and God's work.* Man is a poor, frail, weak, empty thing, and will remain so—*until!* He is indeed "full of sound and fury, signifying *nothing"—until!* Until he is transfigured and magnified and glorified by the One who pours Himself and His Resources through the man. Thus, he becomes the vehicle of God's full self-expression. This is what man was made and meant to be, and this is his greatness. Thus saith the Old Testament. What says the New Testament?

## II. The Magnificence of Man as Seen in the New Testament

Second, we will examine *the magnificence of man as it is seen in the New Testament.* I will isolate the two leaders of the Christian movement and allow them to show us this truth. First, Jesus the Savior, then Paul the leading spokesman for Christ and the Gospel.

First, look at Jesus, *the majestic Master.* Jesus often stated or implied this view of man as God's vehicle. As an example, when He sent out the Twelve to minister to sick and sinful people in the towns and villages of Galilee, knowing full well their weaknesses and unreadiness,

He says plainly to them, "Freely you have received, freely give." The word freely conditions both their receiving and their giving, and the giving is only possible because they have first received. That is, what they have received from Him is what they are to remit to others. Their inventory of resources was comprised of the Divine Message and Miracle(s) Jesus had discipled into them. They are only to be channels, vehicles, pouring out into others what has first been poured into their own experience. That is their calling, their character, their commission, their competence. The same is true of you, dear Christian, and me. You are to give (only) what you have gotten; you are to remit what you have first received. You are commissioned to be a vehicle of God's Grace and Glory.

Furthermore, Jesus said that when persecution comes and they stand before judges, they are not to prepare beforehand what they shall say, or how they will answer the judges. No, the Spirit will speak through them. And when under the very shadow of the Cross, when they gathered in the Upper Room, fearfully facing the unknown but threatening future, the prescription is the same—"Abide in Me, and I in you. If you abide in me, you shall bring forth fruit." And what is fruit, but simply the getting on the outside what is inside the fruit-bearing plant. It is simply overflowing life. The branch is only the vehicle of the life of the vine. "Without Me, you can do nothing." The implication? If you will allow the full and free flow of My Life (a very difficult accomplishment), you can do anything I want done!

Then, on the mountain in Galilee, as He sends them forth to "make disciples in all nations"—yes, even in a brutal world dominated by Rome with all of its potential for force and violence, the message sounds again: *"All authority is given unto Me* in Heaven and on earth"—"Go ye *therefore...*" We are asked to acknowledge it again as the foundation of our lives and actions—we are but channels, *vehicles*, bearers of His Word, conduits of His grace, and "power-points" of His Self-release among needy men. By the way, this is why the Twelve and the early church *had to wait for Pentecost*, where and when God made the full release of His redemptive power among men. And from that Day, the followers of Christ were vehicles of the Glory and Grace of God.

Now, look at Paul, the main ambassador for Christ in Christian history, the man with an incredible capacity as a *vehicle of Christ*. For Paul, too, this vehicle-assignment is the basic assumption about man. Paul's invariable message is that God's people are to ever be the vehicles of energies greater than their own, the very resources of God Himself. Paul also held firmly to the "flip side" of this truth, that man may also be the vehicle of *evil*, vehicles for the expression of sin and Satan. So Paul simply echoes Jesus and all the spokesmen of the Old Testament. Paul's statements about man as God's vehicles are clear and unmistakable. Sometimes his words containing explicit statements such as, "Not I, but the grace of God which is in me," or "I live, yet not I, but Christ lives in me." At other times, this truth is implicit in other statements of Paul, such as, "...according to the power that energizes in us," and "that the life also of Jesus might be manifested in my body," or "we are strengthened with might by His Spirit in the inner man," and "that Christ may dwell ('settle down and be at home, having the run of the house') in your hearts by faith," and "Christ in you, the hope of glory." With this sample array of strategic statements about man as God's vehicle, the case might rest.

Let me repeat what I have said twice earlier. As Paul saw man, man could become by his choice either the vehicle of Satan or of God, the channel either of unholy spirits or of the Holy Spirit, of sin or of grace. Which it would be, a man could/must choose—but he will by virtue of his nature inevitably be one or the other. To be a vehicle, that is man's *glory* or his *gloom*, his *delight* or his *doom*—*and he must choose.* Someone will protest, "Oh, no, I won't be put in a corner; I will remain neutral." Friend, to not choose is to choose not, not to be what you were made and meant to be.

I have not yet stated the greatest Biblical presentation of the fact of man as a vehicle of God's self-expression. I have saved the best picture until last. The entire New Testament message presents the answer to the question, "What is man?" And the answer is unmistakably clear. God's "final answer" is, as always, spelled out (John 1:16) *in Christ.* To see God's view of man forever etched on the pages of history, we turn again to the Unique Son of God. The entire New Testament proclamation is God's answer "shouted loud and clear". The answer is seen in the *Incarnation* of Christ, "Without controversy, great is the mystery of Godliness: God was manifest in human flesh" (I Timothy 3:16). "The Word (Greek, *logos;* meaning, 'logic,' the Logic or the Mind of God, one of the replete titles for Jesus) became flesh, and dwelt among us" (John 1:14). Colossians 2:3 says that "In Him dwell all the riches of wisdom and knowledge." He is the Vehicle of God's Life, God's Love, God's Power—God's total revelation of Himself. "He who has seen Me has seen the Father", i.e., I am a *vehicle* (John 14:9), said the Incarnate God. "The Unique Son, who is in the bosom of the Father, has spelled Him out", said John (John 1:16). Jesus has expressed God, inside-out, as God's own vehicle for communicating Himself.

Here is humanity at its highest, from God's own viewpoint. Here is man's nature, function, and full-time vocation. You see, man's highest destiny is to Christ-like, a vehicle for communicating God into a perverted, puzzled world.

## III. The Message for Us Today

Finally, we will examine the message of this Truth for us today. What are the implications of man as a vehicle of God's Person and Power? First, our *shortcomings* are exposed by this Truth. We often hear today that the modern church *could* practice greater efficiency, *could* utilize greater organization, and *could* employ wider and better marketing techniques, and these are among the proposed panaceas for the many failures and deficiencies of the church. From "consumer friendliness" to "contributing membership", and many others besides, the gamut of remedies is run. Maybe the church has some need for these things, but her real problem and the proposal to meet it are found elsewhere.

The church today needs a radical and vast enlargement of her spiritual capital. The church needs to realize that at her very best, she is only the vehicle of God's Word, God's Plans, and God's Actions. This would assure that the church lives in full dependence upon God, realized in desperate and persistent prayer. Just as the old Moravians had a non-stop one hundred year prayer meeting, the church needs the same today. We must declare—and implement through prayer—our radical need of God. Then, we would be far more responsive to the promptings of the Spirit, far more open to the direction of God, far more expectant of His surprise powerful visits among us, looking for the unpredictable but recognizable work of God among us, watchful for the signs of God's doing new and powerful things among us, and aware that God will require new and radical things from us. When our hearts are thus bent to His will and work, our shortcomings will drive us deeper into His Word and His will. And the church will consciously experience a radical and vast enlargement of her spiritual capital.

Second, we will re-examine and restate the real meaning of *success*. Once we realize our true vocation as vehicles of *God's accomplishment*, we will see that the true meaning of success is not found in popularity, or publicity, or prosperity, or pride in our own achievement, but is defined by the evidences that *GOD is at work among us*. What are the evidences? The Holy Spirit is melting men down right before our eyes. Hearts are broken before Him in a new breakthrough of Eternal Reality, and God is conspicuously enjoying Himself among us. The grace of God is making each of us more gracious, the love of God is making each of us more loving, and the power of God is making each of us more powerful for Him. The power of God is delivering men from sin. Christ is coming to reign in more and more hearts and lives—and all of us are singing in the reign! We would gratefully—*gratefully*—acknowledge this as true success. God has increasingly made us the *vehicles* of His Life on earth.

Third, old conventional, traditional forms of ministry would give way to a new *strategy*. The church would no longer have the profile of being the church when it is *gathered*, but will be proving that it is the church in its *going* (that is, in every step, every word, every deed *outside the place of meeting*) and God would release Himself throughout our communities as His people surrender to be the vehicles of His moment-by-moment release of Himself through them.

Frankly, the church would linger a long time before the Great Commission of Jesus and realize that His *authority and power* preceded the Command in the statement of Jesus, and His *attending Presence* proceeds from the fulfillment of the Commission. Thus, we will test our obedience to the Commission by the show of His authority and power among us and through us, and by the evidences of His attending Presence endorsing us as His vehicles with more and more fruit. In short, the mighty anointing of God would be upon His people once again, and fruit would be vast and certain. Our strategy would be to obey God and His Word—and then get out of His way. We could then stop talking about "revival", which at best is a temporary state anyway, and begin to expect the power of God to remain upon us and move through us as we yield to be His ready vehicles.

Our role as His vehicles? We would seek, and expect, nothing for ourselves (may God help each of us, for this requires a top-drawer miracle). We would ask neither thanks, nor recognition, nor reward—except to know that we pleased Jesus (II Corinthians 5:9; again, may God help us, because each of us lives so much for his own gratification and pleasure, even in spiritual things). We will truly, truly realize that "we have This Treasure (the Lord, the Life, and the Light of the Gospel) in earthen vessels, that the excellency of the power might be of God, and not of us." He will share His rightful glory with no man, and as long as we claim, or think, or insinuate credit for ourselves in His work, we are no long vehicles of His glory. So we must learn to deliberately step aside, and not even to call attention to our "humility" in doing so. Thus, we will let God show His Hand and bare His Arm, and do His own work in His own way—and we must be indifferent as to which human instrument appears at the moment to be the vehicle of it.

Fourth, as we play our full role as God's vehicles, we will find an unshakeable *security, serenity and stability* in the face of any and all challenges—adversity, weakness, frustration, persecution, rejection, etc., etc.—and the challenges will be many and mighty.

Paul was at Ephesus when he wrote the Second Corinthian letter. While in Ephesus, he faced the most intense opposition of his career. He speaks in the Corinthian letter of being "pressed out of measure, beyond strength to endure, despairing even of life." He experienced severe illness as well as a piercing "stake in the flesh", which he identified as "a messenger of Satan to buffet him." Three times he desperately asked God to remove it, but instead of the removal which he requested came a reply about inner Divine resource which was enough ("sufficient for you"). This mighty Divine affirmation rang out with Heaven's gentle but thunderous authority over Paul's circumstance—*"MY GRACE IS SUFFICIENT FOR YOU, FOR MY STRENGTH IS MADE PERFECT IN WEAKNESS."* Paul reaffirmed his role as a vehicle of God's Person and Power when he testified, "Most gladly therefore will I rather (note that word; instead of *what?)* glory in my infirmities, that the power of Christ may rest upon me...for when I am weak, then I am strong." That is, when I am out of the way, and weak enough not to push myself into the spotlight, I am confident that You will show Yourself strong in my/our/their behalf.

Friends, very few believers ever walk that spiritually elite pathway. Eternity will reveal God's appreciation of them. Yet this is the ultimate truth about man—about you and me. We are vehicles only, agents and channels of the Eternal God, elevated by the cause we serve and the role we play, and enriched by the Person and power that flow through us.

"Channels only, Blessed Master,
But with all Your grace and power
Flowing through us, You can use us,
Every day and every hour."

"Out in the highways and by-ways of life, Many are weary and sad;
Carry the Son-shine where darkness is rife, Making the sorrowing glad.
Tell the sweet story of Christ and His love, Tell of His power to forgive;
Others will trust Him if only you prove True, every moment you live.
Give as it was given to you in your need, Love as the Master loved you;
Be to the helpless a helper indeed, Unto your mission be true.
Make me a blessing, make me a blessing, Out of my life may Jesus shine;
Make me a blessing, O Savior, I pray, Make me a blessing to someone today."

For additional copies contact us at:
***Spiritual Life Ministries***
2916 Old Elm Lane
Germantown, TN 38138
(901) 758-2777
Email: herbslm@mindspring.com

# Chapter Outlines

## Chapter 1 -- The Meaning of Man

*I. Understand His Person*

*II. Understand His Purpose*

*III. Understand His Progress*

*IV. Understand His Potential*

## Chapter 2 -- The Making of Man

*I. The Sequence of Man's Creation*

*II. The Seriousness of Man's Creation*

*III. The Substance of the One Created*

*IV. The Splendor of His Character*

## Chapter 3 -- The Marriage and Mating of Man

*I. The Provision for the Mate and the Marriage*

*II. The Preparation of the Mate for the Marriage*

*III. The Purposes of the Mate and the Marriage*

*IV. The Personal Role of the Mate*

*V. The Divine Prescription for a Biblical Marriage*

## Chapter 4 -- The Makeup of Man

*I. God's Design of Man*

*II. God's Dilemma with Man*

*III. God's Desire for Man*

## Chapter 5 -- The Misery of Man

*I. The Circumstances of the Misery of Man*

*II. The Components of the Misery of Man*

*III. The Cure for the Misery of Man*

## Chapter 6 -- The Measure of Man

*I. The Individual Standard of Self-Measurement*

*II. The Interpersonal Standard of Society's Measurement*

*III. The Ideal Standard of the Savior's Measurement*

## Chapter 7 -- Mercy for Man

*I. The Record of Sin in Human Experience*

*II. The Removal of Sin and Its Record from Human Experience*

*III. The Replacement of the Record of Sin in Human Experience*

## Chapter 8 -- A Master for Man

*I. The Fact of Christ's Lordship*

*II. The Foundation of Christ's Lordship*

*III. The Force of Christ's Lordship*

## Chapter 9 -- The Magnitude of Man

*I. Formed by God*

*II. Deformed by Guilt*

*III. Transformed by Grace*

*IV. Conformed in Glory*

## Chapter 10 -- A Motto for Man – Christianity Condensed

*I. The Christian Life Is Deeply Personal*

*II. The Christian Life Is Wonderfully Practical*

*III. The Christian Life Is Gloriously Possible*

*IV. The Christian Life Is Eternally Profitable*

## Chapter 11 -- So, What Is Man?

*I. The Meaning of Man As Seen in the Old Testament*

*II. The Magnificence of Man As Seen in the New Testament*

*III. The Message for Us Today*